the rules of attraction

the rules of attraction

Fourteen practical rules to help get the right clients, talent and resources to COME TO YOU!

MARK DEO

New York

The Rules of Attraction

Fourteen Practical Rules to get the right clients, talent and resources to come to you!

ISBN 978-1-60037-564-4

MORGAN · JAMES
THE ENTREPRENEURIAL PUBLISHER

Morgan James Publishing, LLC
1225 Franklin Ave., STE 325
Garden City, NY 11530-1693
Toll Free 800-485-4943
www.MorganJamesPublishing.com

Dedication

The Rules of Attraction is dedicated to my wife, Kathleen who endured my continual vacillating about what I should or should not include in this book. Through all this she patiently encouraged me and helped me to stay focused on the central theme and suggested how many others could benefit from the concepts included in these pages.

Table of Contents

Foreword

It happens often: a term or a concept enters the cultural consciousness so quickly that its power and trueness becomes lost in comfortable idiom. So it has been with the force of "attraction," which I believe is not only one of the most over-simplified principles in business today, but also one of the most misunderstood concepts in the context of client development and the building of business relationships. Since Rhonda Byrne's mega-successful project *The Secret,* the concept of "attraction," once primarily associated with the physical aspects of personal relationships, has become a kind of cultural panacea for the "name it and claim it" mentality of attracting wealth and prosperity. From James Arthur's financial advisement to Joel Osteen's spiritual guidance, millions of readers have been themselves attracted to the idea that if I walk, talk, and think like a Trump, then I'll one day magically become a Trump (sans hair, of course).

Nothing could be further from the truth.

Attracting the success one seeks requires more than affirmation and vision statements. This is never more true than it is among those who work daily to build and grow small businesses: these entrepreneurs seek tools, not tricks. But few of the pundits who pontificate about attraction provide a realistic formula for creating client attraction in a typical small business environment. After reviewing more than one hundred of the top-selling books that claim to show readers how to attract more business, I found *not one* of those books tells the reader precisely how to go about applying the vague concept of attraction specifically to the small business model. In fact, most of these books espouse the same traditional marketing concepts—the five P's of marketing (People, Price, Product, Promotion, and Place), for instance—which have been found to produce the opposite of the intended effect: pushing customers further away, rather than attracting them.

This book does not seek to add itself to those numbers. To my knowledge, there has never been a book that has been dedicated exclusively to the concept of attraction as it applies to *practical client development* and, more specifically, to getting better results from entrepreneurial marketing initiatives. In the last few decades, numerous marketing books have been written about what other successful organizations have done to create an attractive brand or a better customer experience. I myself have been educated and influenced by many of these works. Yet nearly all of them focus on the pursuit of traditional marketing; attraction-based marketing principles are typically presented in static generalizations. No matter how inspiring, none of them truly answer "How do I apply this concept to my business?" And so readers are left scratching their heads.

The *Rules of Attraction* takes the reader on a step-by-step journey that not only educates them on the principles of attraction but also inspires them to put those guiding rules into action. By demonstrating the way each rule works in specific marketing initiatives, the *Rules of Attraction* is the *only* book that includes specific exercises that demonstrate how to implement each of the fourteen rules in *any* type of business, large or small, new or old, well-financed or poorly-funded. My aim: to leave no one scratching his head.

Acknowledgements

This book is the culmination of decades of experience in marketing just about every type of product or service imaginable: professional services, manufacturing, high technology, construction, real estate, financial products, consumer goods, transportation services, retail and more. I've found that, across nearly every industry, the principles of marketing remain the same. Few business authors have focused on the practical step-by-step approach to mastering these principles in a marketing or branding strategy, and I understand why: it's difficult! I would not have been able to even begin to recount this methodology without the education, inspiration, and encouragement of hundreds of people whom I have had the honor of knowing and working with. As such, this book is a collaborative work.

First I would like to thank my wife Kathleen who has endured me for nearly a quarter century. She has heard every story in this book thousands of times and to this day still acts interested, even amazed, every time I tell them. Now that is love!

Next, I would like to thank my most senior team member, Matt Walker, who helped to write some of the stories in this book, and so is, in a sense, my co-author. For ten years Matt was the co-host of my CBS radio show, The Small Business Hour. He joined in my enthusiasm regarding this project and helped me make this book a reality. In addition, he worked tirelessly on the Web site, the "Attract More Business Learning Program," and dealt with my moods, for which he is to be greatly commended.

I would also like to thank my partner for over 20 years in this consortium, Max Parker. He is a creative genius. Not only is he responsible for the visuals in this book, but his excellent team of designers have worked to bring about many of the marketing successes you will read about in these pages. Since design is critical to the success of any branding or marketing attraction strategy, Max has over the years taught me to recognize exceptional design and never to settle for mediocre imagery. These lessons have not only allowed us to make hundreds of millions of dollars for our clients but have set SBA Network, Inc. apart from the many typical marketing agencies nationwide.

In addition I would like to thank Cory Halbardier who, as my future successor, has helped me to become a better leader and more effective marketer. While he is young, he has progressed more in the few years we have worked together than I have in a decade. I have never worked with a person that could absorb and put into practice these rules so quickly and creatively. Without his inspiration and friendly goading, this book would not have become a reality.

I would be remiss to forget to mention the many clients over the years who have placed their confidence in me and our group by retaining us and allowing us to implement the Rules of Attraction in their businesses. Their commitment and trust in our abilities have been an honor. They were willing to risk their entire company, brand, and reputation on what at the time was an "unproven" strategy. They have not only helped us to create a profitable property, but have also instilled confidence and self-meaning into our work. Special thanks to: Ian Mitchell, Bill and Lorraine Flegenheimer, Patty and Mike Blum.

Finally I would like to extend my deepest thanks for the many coaches, teachers, and mentors that have helped me to learn the foundational truths that eventually resulted in my creating the Rules of

Attraction and that allowed me to adapt them to many diverse marketing challenges. Without their guidance and honesty this book would never have come to pass. Special thanks to: Morrie and Arlea Shechtman of Fifth Wave Leadership, Tom Kiblen of Dale Carnegie Training, Stewart Greenberg of Yamaha International, Suzanne Schneider of Walker Group International, Ivo Rabbison of Nikko Electronics, Kenyu Asamoto of ASTI Pacific, Seth Godin, Tim Sanders, Jay Abraham, and of course, Joseph Deo, my father.

Introduction

A world with less friction

The Principle of Attraction

Imagine this.

You are a gazelle. In the grassy savannas of Africa, your eyes scan the wide horizon as a dry wind moves across the landscape.

A rustling. Sudden movement in the margins of your sight. A blur of brown and white. And there you are: face-to-face with a bloodthirsty, hungry lion.

What do you do?

Run like the wind, blood pumping in your veins. Lungs nearly exploding. Run faster and harder with fear in your heart, leaping, darting, your legs springing you forward toward the distant sun. One thought haunts you: the lion does not tire easily. She will chase you until you tire, until you stumble from exhaustion. And then…

Suddenly the chase is interrupted. Mere yards from your legs, the lion's teeth have been drawn away—distracted by an older, slower, less agile gazelle. The pride descends upon the fated beast, and you live to see another day.

Later, as you graze upon the same plain—not fifty yards from the very same lion and her indomitable pride—you watch as the beasts recline beneath the Eucalyptus trees. Your eyes meet your former huntress. She blinks in the brilliant sun. You take a few steps toward her, and bow your head to eat. You are no longer afraid.

Why?

In the current paradigm, it is assumed that business is still about pursuit: we are all of us either the hunter or the hunted. Standard marketing tools use well-known maneuvers to trick or trap one's prey: the customer. In the battle among competing predators, there is always a winner and a loser. We battle for share of market and share of mind, and somebody goes home hungry.

Traditional business practices have, for the most part, remained self-centered and manipulative, designed with one goal in mind: to get someone to do exactly what you want them to do: buy your product or service, perform the task you outlined, take the actions that you deem important.

In this model, there's no question who the customer is: the fated gazelle. Wandering an open territory, waiting for the next marketing beast to trip them up. In my years as a consultant, I have found that customers are not ignorant to this implied metaphor; they know exactly how they're seen, and they feel very much like they are being hunted, stalked, and eventually chased down. They feel that way because it's become the accepted norm that those of us selling products or offering services are lions, and to get what we want, we have to act hungry, move aggressively, hope there's a slow-footed gazelle in the group, and hope that we beat the rest of the lions to the meal. Most business owners will tell you this is an exhausting and inefficient process. But until now, it's simply the only model they've had.

But let's ask the most powerful question at our disposal: *what if?* What if we were able to break out of the predatorial paradigm? What if we were able to present our ideas or solutions in such a way that people sought us out, rather than us having to chase after them? What if we could market in such a way that our customers *chose* our company, product, or service over the competition? What if team members and business partners decided, on their own, that they *wanted* to work efficiently and rightly instead of our having again and again to correct their behavior?

In other words, what if we could develop a deep, indisputable *attraction*?

How valuable would it be to your business if you could attract the right kind of employees, affiliate relationships, alliances…even customers? Imagine attracting your ideal prospect without spending a dime on advertising or an hour for a sales pitch!

Most marketing communication expresses a similar theme: what a company, product, or service *does*. At best, marketing materials may promise some generic group of benefits in which buyers *may* be interested. Even the best and most effective of these materials (Web sites, brochures, flyers, ads, radio or TV spots, promotions, interactive CDs or videos) attempt to communicate to the customer why a given product, service, or company is better than the competition. So most of us sweat out our days on the savannah, hoping not to go to bed hungry.

Too rarely do we focus on the *problem* that the customer is having. Few have designed solutions that are so customized to their target audience that listeners, readers, or buyers would have to be insane even to consider another option. Discovering and addressing the customer's problem is at the core of the attraction mindset.

Greed is Good. NOT!

These three images on the front page of the *New York Times* were so memorable I clipped and filed them immediately.

Five Enron directors, hands upraised, swear to a Senate subcommittee that they were not responsible for the company's collapse. They looked so brave and innocent.

America's favorite homemaker (and cake-baker and basket weaver), Martha Stewart, spends months in prison after being convicted of lying to investigators about why she sold thousands of shares of stock just before the price plunged on a negative government report. Darn those coincidences.

And the President of the United States is impeached due to a series of unfortunate prevarications. Politics, many say, as usual.

Profit. Gain. Power. Wealth. Greed. The mantras of our American Empire.

The American economic ethos has, until now, measured the health of an organization and the success of its leaders by single quantifier: the numbers. It all boils down to the numbers.

Or does it?

Ms. Stewart's turnaround has been exceptional, deliberately softening her image and rebuilding her intangible assets by winning the respect of even her most dour critics. The result? Her net worth and stock prices have soared, and her endorsements have increased dramatically.

Former President Clinton's mistakes have faded into hazy memories, overshadowed by the generosity of the William Jefferson Clinton Foundation, his work with tsunami relief, and the celebration of his new book. Its title: *Giving*.

The Enron icons, however, have showed no signs of greater redemption.

Today's mantras are of a different sort. Corporate governance. Social responsibility. Economic democracy. Business ethics is the topic of the day. Remember Michael Douglas in *Wall Street*? "Greed is good," he preached. "Greed in all its forms."

And he was convincing: we admired Gordon Gekko and his ruthless approach—some of us secretly wanted to be like him. (I know I did!) Now two decades removed from the release of Oliver Stone's film, financial moguls such as Henry Kravis (creator of the leveraged buyout), Michael Milken, and Ivan Boesky have made billions on corporate raiding and hostile takeovers. And while many thought that the "greed is good" attitude of the 80s would end, Wall Street has seen even more takeovers in the last two decades and initial public offerings have been more lucrative than ever.

So what's changed between then and now? In the new millennium, today's tycoons and power players have gained a much softer image by using less hostile actions and focusing more on intangibles. In his autobiography, Donald Trump, this generation's icon of capitalism, states quite simply, "money no longer interests me very much. I'm more motivated by the challenge of a deal and the impact on others." His frankness is refreshing. The financial mavens of our new age have begun to realize that in order to preserve wealth and enhance value they must focus on more than simply "the numbers."

Not that the Donald has gone all touchy-feely on us. But he has realized his image benefits from softening. And it's not just the "Donald" that has bought into this concept. Bill Gates and Warren Buffett have locked arms and deeded billions of their collective personal fortunes to create the world's richest charitable foundation. The wolfs of Wall Street may be lamenting, but being a ruthless capitalist pig is now passé. Business practices that lack transparency, that are only about how the major players will benefit, are no longer the most effective.

The Times They Are A-Changin'

The success of Barack Obama in winning the presidency on November 4, 2008 owes much to his message like the promise to pass Democratic policies by rallying a "coalition for change." But watching Obamamania take hold during his campaigning it became rather apparent that something more subtle was at work. While I am not a supporter of Mr. Obama's policies, I must say I was quite impressed at the way the campaign unfolded with a compelling brand and a smooth, systemic viral marketing effort. All this was reinforced with a coherent, comprehensive program of fonts, logos, slogans, Web design and strategically placed advertisements and announcements. Obama was the first presidential candidate to be marketed like a high-end consumer brand.

Mr. Obama clearly won the presidency with a well-crafted attraction-based marketing campaign wrapped around one word... CHANGE.

And no one can deny that change is upon us. Not only are we experiencing more change— environmentally, technologically, politically, socially, economically and even interpersonally—today than ever before in history, but the rate at which change is occurring is accelerating as well. Scientific knowledge doubles every fifteen years, and the reservoir of print knowledge doubles every eight. The average young adult today must manage more relationships in one year than their grandparents had to manage during their entire lives. Obviously, a business owner must not wonder if he or she will face major change in the coming months. The more important question is: "How will I deal with it?"

If we approach change from the standpoint of attraction, then we won't simply struggle to adapt to uncontrollable change; instead, we can *lead* revolutionary change! With the right knowledge, mindset, and discipline, we can actually attract positive, desirable change, rather than being swept away by forces outside of our control.

This kind of "change leadership" requires thinking, acting, and speaking differently. Enter the ***Rules of Attraction:*** 14 guidelines that will move you to the front of the curve.

The Rules of Attraction

1. Become a bigger fish in a smaller pond.
2. Make the problem more important than the solution.
3. Create an exclusive community of "super-users."
4. Be the only solution.
5. Reject strategically.
6. Give information away.
7. Reverse people's risk.
8. Let design and color speak.
9. Win heartshare.
10. Collaborate rather than compete.
11. Who we are is more important than what we do.
12. Create standards and systems that nurture growth.
13. Learn the discipline of testing.
14. Destroy your business.

In some of these rules, you may recognize behavior or thought patterns you follow instinctively. In other cases, perhaps you have even consciously applied some of these concepts. The power of the rules, however, is most effectively set into motion when we *internalize* them. When we make these rules part of who we are, we find that we are using them without even thinking about them, and thus become "unconsciously competent." When this happens, we can *lead* positive change on a massive scale in all circumstances and across all relationships.

Toward a Friction-less World

Transport yourself back to high school and plant yourself in Mr. Simmons' Physics class. On the blackboard is written in all caps: FRICTION.

Crash course: Friction appears whenever two objects rub against each other. Although an object might appear smooth, on a microscopic level it is very rough and jagged. When two objects rub against each other: voila! *Friction*. Friction's a stubborn force, contrary by nature. No matter which direction an object moves, friction pulls the other way. Move something left, friction pulls right. Move something up, friction pulls down. Think about this long enough and one is convinced that nature was designed to make things stay exactly where they are.

Friction not just a scientific concept, so feel free to step out of the classroom. Friction is a relational term as well: when one person's perception differs from another's there is "relationship friction." Friction is an economic term, too: it's the sticky area of a business or industry, like the security line at an airport, in which new concerns and demands rub up against current ability. Typically, friction is inversely proportionate to the amount of change we want to produce. For example, if you're looking to launch a new product, you might follow a typical approach: design and print product announcements and send them to customers, develop press kits and send them to the media in hopes of getting published product reviews. These actions are not incorrect, but they will unavoidably create *friction*. First, the customers who receive the announcement might say; "my supplier is just looking for a way to sell me more products at a higher price." The resistance created by that cynicism is friction. Or perhaps the media that receives the press kit might have so many press materials to review that there is just not enough time to do so. The glut of material slows down the speed at which your product gains exposure: again, friction. In other words, the time required to review all the press material or the investment required to buy the new product rubs up against the perception of the potential value gained.

This force operates in the world of management as well as marketing. I recently met with a company that was experiencing a steep reduction in customer satisfaction levels. They obviously needed to change the way their customer service representatives were handling client issues. The traditional approach: launch a customer service training initiative. Not a bad idea. But they needed to recognize the friction that any kind of initiatives would create. In this case, the customer service staff will need to commit the time to attend the training. That time commitment would rub against the time that would have been dedicated to assisting customers. And there it is: friction.

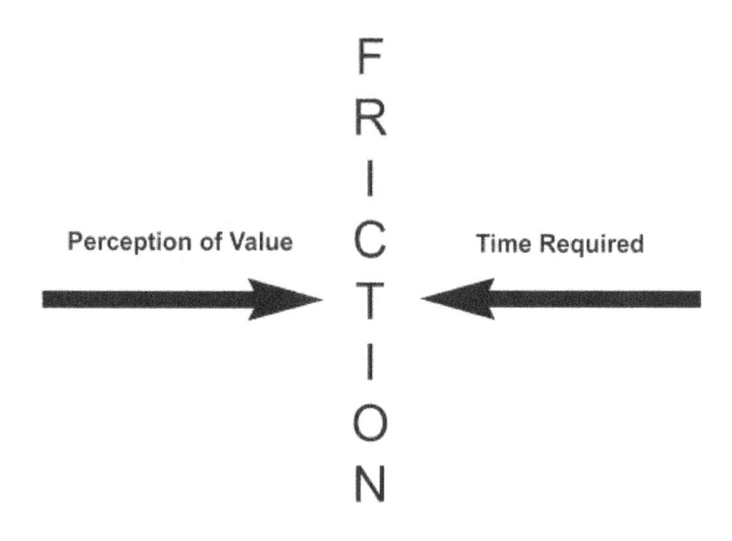

Whether we are attempting to bring about change with prospects/clients in the marketplace or employees/shareholders in management, the force of attraction is the fastest way to bring about change for one simple reason: it creates a world with very little friction. While friction can never be completely eliminated, the rules of attraction allow us to reduce significantly friction and create positive perceptions. In marketing, for example, when we understand the client's challenges better than the competition does, we automatically become more attractive. In a management setting, the more we understand the employee's problems the more we are able to customize solutions to their needs. Merely understanding and empathizing with the problem reduces friction. Another way to reduce friction is to become a more targeted and exclusive solution to the customer's problem. As we will see later in this book, doing this is particularly critical in business relationships today. By isolating a particular market with particular needs we are often able to create solutions that no one else can.

An Invitation to Attract

As we look at each of the fourteen rules of attraction, we'll discover how others, from leaders of Fortune 100 companies to independent professionals, have utilized these same principles specifically to make themselves and their companies more attractive. We will see how they have been able to not just win greater market share or even mind share but greater *heartshare*. And we will see how, surprisingly, focusing on *destruction* can often bring greater growth to businesses, products, and services than the traditional business development techniques.

One early warning: you may find many of the principles presented in this book counterintuitive. They may go against what you were taught in business school or what you learned from senior managers. Be not afraid! Today's business environment presents challenges that have never before been experienced, and if we do not begin dealing with these challenges with a different set of tools, we are destined never to realize our full potential. Without new paradigms, new sets of skills, new problem-solving techniques, and new visions, we will continue to see more than fifty percent of all business start-ups fail. The flip-side: if we are willing to unlearn the old ways, to relearn relationships, and to re-imagine the forces of attraction, our companies, products, relationships, and service will not only see continuing growth but also will create greater value for our clients, employees, shareholders, families, and for ourselves well into the future.

Imagine this.

You are a gazelle. In the grassy savannas of Africa, you have just escaped the roar and rage of a lioness and her pride.

Later, as you graze upon the same plain—not fifty yards from the very same lions—you watch as the beasts recline beneath the trees. Your eyes meet your former huntress. She blinks in the brilliant sun. You take a few steps toward her, and bow your head to eat. You are no longer afraid. Because the lions are no longer acting hungry.

Rule #1:

Become a Bigger Fish in a Smaller Pond

Ann the Crab

In my home in California, my family keeps a red-river crab named Ann, who is quite special to us. You're probably thinking, "Who has a pet crab?" Well, we do. Let me explain.

One evening while dining at our favorite Japanese sushi bar (*everyone* in L.A. has a favorite sushi bar), the chef brought out some small live crabs and set them on the counter. One crab sidled over to my wife and seemed to look up at her and say, "Please don't eat me. Take me home. I'll give you love!"

Perhaps it was compassion, or perhaps it was too much sake, that prompted my wife to agree to take Ann home—along with several other crabs that the chef insisted we adopt (and you always listen to the chef at your favorite sushi place!). We placed them all in a large aquarium, which we decorated with rocks and seaweed, and watched as they all proceeded to die, until only one was left: our beloved Ann.

Fearing she'd have a few morbid memories of the fish tank, we relocated Ann, placing her in a glass flower vase with a few rocks. Call me a pessimist, but I expected her to die as well. To our surprise, not only did Ann survive, she actually *thrived*! Over the next few weeks, she began to eat better (of course, she had all the food to herself). She grew more social–that's right, a crab can be social. She has even molted; that is, she threw off her shell and grew a new one, something crabs do only when they feel at home in an established habitat. Though a red-river crab has a typical lifespan of four to six months, we just celebrated Ann's first birthday. Our sushi chef is amazed.

Ann is *outside* the curve. We think it's because we have helped create for her a unique environment that perfectly suits her needs. She was much happier as a bigger fish in a smaller pond—or should I say, a bigger crab in a smaller vase.

It's not just true for crabs. Customers want to feel that what we're offering is perfectly suited to them, that our solution matches their needs. They want to feel that they are the only game in town.

Beyond Niche Marketing

Because of my profession as a consultant, broadcaster, and teacher, I engage with many business leaders from many different industry positions. Nearly every person I meet, regardless of their industry or profession, tells me the same thing: "My business is different." They feel that their industry has special needs and challenges, that technology has changed the landscape of their profession in a unique way. They feel that price is of greater importance than ever before. They believe that they now have more competitors than at any other time in history. And they all say this with genuine concern and the honest belief that these challenges are exclusive to *their* industry or profession.

The fact is that nearly *every* product and service category has been affected by technology, price erosion, and increased competition. Good news: you're not alone.

There are more competitors emerging every day in every industry and profession. Because of this, we might find ourselves chasing *any* type of business that we can get. In a highly competitive environment, there is a tremendous temptation to take "whatever comes along" until you find some kind of niche. This strategy is no longer effective—if it ever was.

While you are taking whatever comes along, so are the rest of your competitors. This aimless process pushes down the market price of the products and services and ultimately results in price erosion—and worse, it creates technology or price wars wherein the weakest players are eliminated. With so many wandering like this, it's not surprising that U.S. Department of Commerce states that ninety percent of all new businesses fail in their first year.

Avoid being part of that dire statistic. Rule #1: *Become a Bigger Fish in a Smaller Pond.* Far more important than identifying a market niche—i.e., the kind of business you want—is identifying the kind of business that you ***do not*** want. And that starts by fully understanding the marketplace in which we compete.

Standing in the Gap

A word from Sun Tzu, the ancient Chinese warrior: "If you know the enemy and know yourself, your victory will not stand in doubt."

While I am not suggesting that we look at our competitors as our enemies—in fact, later in this book we will look at the value of collaboration with our competitors—there's no substitute for knowing the landscape, whether of battle or business. A thorough competitive analysis is a must for every entrepreneur. Only by fully mapping the competitive topography can you see how your company, product, or service integrates into it, and thereby identify the *gap* in the marketplace that will be the site of your conquest.

The ***gap*** is the area of product, service, quality, selection, application, delivery or price that is not currently being satisfied. When you understand the gap in the market you can find the specialized need or needs which you can *exclusively* satisfy. If you develop your product to satisfy the gap, you have the ability to define a very tightly focused audience profile. This audience then becomes your exclusive focus. This is a commitment to extreme specialization: you will only accept business that matches the profile of the type of customer you want to deal with. In order to ensure that your product or service matches the specific unmet needs of the target market—the gap—it is critical that we invest time in fully understanding our competition.

The best way—completely ethical and devastatingly effective—to understand your competition is to *become their customer*. Though few entrepreneurs or business professionals do this, becoming a customer of your competition is the single best way to understand them. Call them. Visit them. Send e-mails. Ask lots of questions. Do not tell them you are a competitor; your purpose is to learn what makes them tick.

The Competitive Landscape Profile

In our consulting firm, the "Competitive Landscape Profile," or the CLP, is one tool we use to understand our client's competitors. The CLP allows us to plot the proficiency of each of our competitors—and it gives us a very clear picture of who they are, what they do, where they fit, and how they are different. When completed, the CLP locates the gap as clearly as a compass points north.

In the Sample CLP chart below, I have identified the types of competitors that provide marketing services, and I have listed some of the variables that differentiate these types of competitors. Then I have rated their performance in each area. As the arrows at the bottom of the page show, the competitors that should be targeted are the independent consultants and the in-house providers, because they have a lower position in the market, offer little differentiation, and are not strongly branded. These deficiencies make them competitors whom I term more *palatable*.

Competitive Information Needed

- Advertising: Archive competitors ads and track where and when they advertise as well as what they say in their advertising
- Price list
- Brochure and promotional material: e.g., Point of Purchase material, mailers, packaging, etc.
- Commit their names to memory
- Research the names of their best clients
- Research who the people are that run the company
- Recognize areas where you can cooperate

Competitive Landscape Profile
(for a marketing firm)

Market Variables	Local Consultant	Ad Agency	Nat'l Firms	Promotion Company	In-House Staff
Market Position	Low	High	High	High	Low
Pricing	Low	High	High	High	Low
Customer Service	High	Low	Mid	High	Low
Client Profile	Specialized	Diverse	Diverse	Diverse	Specialized
Product Differentiation	Low	Low	Low	Low	Low
Branding Strategy	Low	High	High	High	Low

Target Practice

Aiming specifically for the gap means behaving in sometimes counterintuitive ways. By rejecting clients that do not precisely meet your criteria, you'll become more attractive to those that do! It works for every type of industry, business, or profession. An example: Sam Walton. Wal-Mart became the largest retailer in America by locating stores where no sane retailer would dare venture. Wal-Mart's even headquartered in the surprising location of Bentonville, Arkansas. Their entire strategy: to target small towns and become not simply another retailer, but in many cases, the *only* retailer in town!

Thankfully, this strategy doesn't only work for multinational giants: it's equally as effective for small businesses, too. I know a financial consultant who works *only* with teachers. That might sound ridiculous, but teachers have very specialized financial needs: they exclusively qualify for special tax treatment, a larger share of their assets can be sheltered, and they often have two sources of income—teaching and summer jobs or a side business. This requires specialized knowledge and advice. My friend has become an expert (big fish) in the area of financial consulting for teachers (small pond).

Even the IRS has entered into the world of specialization, having recently announced their "Market Segment Specialization Program" which develops highly-trained examiners for each particular market segment. A market segment may be an industry such as construction or entertainment, a profession like attorneys or real estate agents, or an issue like passive activity losses. An integral part of the approach is the development and publication of Audit Techniques Guides. These guides contain examination techniques, common and unique industry issues, business practices, industry terminology, and other information to assist examiners in performing examinations. Contain your joy. Just what we need: tax cops with vertical industry knowledge!

Professionals such as doctors and lawyers have been specialists for years. Today you would be hard-pressed to find a doctor that claims to know how to treat all types of illnesses. In fact, it's difficult to get an answer on health issues from only one doctor. These days, even specialists refer patients to specialists.

Regardless of your profession or industry, you can (and should) perform research to help develop a more targeted audience. The more we understand all of the players in the marketplace and where the gaps in quality, service, and delivery lie, the easier it is to identify a vertical market. There are some tremendous resources for this today:

- Vertical industry publications or trade magazines
- The Lifestyles Market Analyst
- FIND/SVP - Nexus/Lexus
- Google
- Hoover's

Oh, and an added bonus to this strategy: in your research, you will undoubtedly come across many prospects that fit your profile.

How I Found the Gap and Narrowed My Own Market:

In the early '90s, my consulting firm made the decision to specialize in specific industry areas. One of the first areas we selected: the cosmetic surgery field. We had an interest in the industry, and living in L.A., more than a solid hunch that this would be a profitable area. So we launched an exhaustive research effort to learn everything we could about cosmetic surgery. We purchased several research studies for a few hundred dollars. I remember the agency we purchased them from told me that I was one of only 12 people that had purchased the 2600 page study. This gave us an inordinate amount of information about the history of the industry, where it was heading, the most popular forms of surgery, technological advancements, changes in the demographics and psychographics of patients electing surgery, practice management issues, insurance and managed care issues, and the potential reduction in the associated costs that were predicted.

Additionally, we interviewed 30 different physicians and learned about their perceptions. We even talked to the president of the American

Medical Association and invited him on our Small Business Hour radio show. (Although they would have been great customers, we did not pitch any of these doctors.) With all the information we gained, we were able to write several articles relying on a variety of statistics about the future of various forms of cosmetic surgery. We were able to speak intelligently on every area of this field. We became more knowledgeable in marketing and managing a cosmetic surgery practice than plastic surgeons themselves. Because of months of research and a few hundred dollars, we were soon viewed as the experts in cosmetic surgery practice management and marketing. Asked to attend a medical conference in Sacramento, I gave a speech on the future of cosmetic surgery. The response was immediate and remarkable. Sixty days before, I would most likely have misspelled "liposuction," and now I was treated as an expert. After seminars on practice management and marketing, editorial contributions to the industries trade publication, and a radio show with the massive pharmaceutical companies Pfizer and Merck for eighteen months on CBS radio, we had established ourselves as the biggest fish in the pond. And this was long before the TV rage of "Extreme Makeover, "Nip/Tuck," and all of the reality show follow-ups. We had pre-empted the trend.

As you can imagine, we were able to attract some of the most successful, well-financed, and well-respected cosmetic surgery clients in the industry in just a few short months. Companies like Sword Medical Center, Cedars Sinai Hospital, Plastico, Boston Medical, and Cosmetic and Laser Surgery all came to us.

No cold calls, no mailings, no fancy brochures. No running after customers. They came running after us. The essence of the attraction principle.

Can you do the same? Yes!

What keeps organizations from narrowing their market? Many remain so focused on the state of their marketplace today that they do not develop a business model that meets the emerging needs of that market. A lack of market perception and understanding of market trends is common even among those in business for many years. Most businesses survive by sheer momentum. They entered the marketplace when their business model was immature and captured a sufficient share of the market for their target area. As a result, many have achieved a degree of success over time. They acquired loyal customers and partners, and their business has grown primarily based on referrals.

This momentum has sustained them for a period of years—maybe even decades. Yet as the business model for their industry begins to change, their market share will lessen. The smart players either radically alter their business model or sell-out while they are at the top and move on to the next rage. But without modifying their business model to adapt to the new market conditions they will ultimately fail, having built their house on shifting sand.

Survival for Start-ups

Of course, in a new start-up, there is no momentum. There aren't many referrals, if any. There aren't partners. There aren't even any customers! So to survive, the startup patterns itself after existing business models—typically, the most successful market leader. The problem with this strategy is that the market leader is likely at the top of the curve in market momentum and has nowhere to go but—you guessed it, DOWN. So the start-up is basing their entire strategy on a model that is at its peak and heading for declination.

Creating an attraction–based start-up strategy can help us to avoid this fatal error. Like attraction-based marketing, attraction-based business start-up management is focused on finding the gap in the marketplace. As discussed earlier, the gap is the business model that is both competitively innovative and closely matches emerging client needs.

By understanding all of the players in the marketplace and identifying their respective business models we clearly identify the laggards, market leaders, and vanguards so we can select the correct business model, rather than one in decline or one so esoteric that its appeal is limited. We must be willing to become more specialized than ever before.

The key to big business is thinking small.

Regardless of whether you are a start-up or a mature business, it is critical that you place a significant priority on finding a way to narrow your audience. The smaller, more tightly confined your marketplace, the better your chances for success. Locate the smallest healthy pond you can find. Then gain some weight and dive in.

Personal Action Plan:

- Who are the best clients for your business? Why?
- What makes them good prospects?
- What are some potential target markets that match with these profiles? Why?
- How can you use this rule to reduce "friction" in your business relationships?
- Choose your target audience based on their revenue needs and budget capabilities.
- Create Your CLP using the form provided on our website at www.markdeo.com/rulesofattraction
- Choose your target audience based on you own interests.
- Choose the type of people with which you like to do business.
- Quality is far more important than quantity.
- Choose one target audience first. Work on penetrating that audience for one year before moving on. You cannot be everything to everyone.

Rule #2:

Make the Problem
More Important Than the Solution

Become the Problem

McDonald's has recently had their entire fleet of trucks painted. Did they put a picture of a Big Mac or Quarter Pounder on the side of the trailer? No. Splashed all over the 18 wheeler is an image of succulent, fresh fruit. What's more odd is that they are now serving granola.

It's true. It took me a while to adjust to this, and the first time I saw it on the menu, I nearly had a heart attack. Which is the opposite of their intent, I suppose. They're not alone in this menu revolution. Arby's has now yogurt. And even Jack-in-the-Box has fresh fruit.

So what the hell is going on here? Burger King introduced the "Have it Your Way *Healthy* Options," McDonald's launched their "Balanced, Active Lifestyles Initiative" and even Sesame Street is crumbling to a healthy diet with Cookie Monster's "A Cookie is a *Sometimes* Food."

Nothing's more all-American than fast food, and our nation's citizens have long loved digging into a bucket of chicken, chomping on a Big Mac, downing a Whopper. How then did the food pyramid ever find its way into the drive-thru?

It's not because consumers have demanded a healthier diet from fast food operators. And it's not because the Federal government is forcing fast food operators to plan healthy menus. No, the fast food giants have discovered one simple truth that forced them to adjust their branding and menu offerings: serving healthier food is simply more profitable.

Let me introduce you to Morgan Spurlock, an eccentric little man who intimidated a multi-billion dollar industry to change their entire business strategy and wiped the smile right off the Happy Meal with "Supersize Me."

How did he do it? How did he bring about such large-scale change? He used the second Rule of Attraction: he focused on the problem—in fact, he *became* the problem. He decided to eat *only* McDonalds for every meal for 30 days to see what would happen. A mix of curiosity and daredevilry led him nearly to kill himself. He gained 30lbs. His blood pressure soared. His cholesterol went through the roof, while his lipids and liver enzymes were at all-time danger levels. He even developed NASH (non-alcoholic steototic hepatitis). Nice job Morgan!

But as a result of his findings and *presentation*, fast food operators were forced to make a change. While it's obvious that McDonald's and their competitors had some work to do on their menu, it was Morgan's manner of procession that got that work done. How successful would Morgan have been if he had gone to the fast food giant with a solution to the problem? What would have resulted from his lobbying congress? Or writing letters to the FDA? Or creating a study for the company stating the positive effects of changing their menu to healthy alternatives? My bet is you'd never have heard of Morgan, and McDonald's would never have heard of the fruit and walnut salad.

Grassroots movements can work—don't get me wrong. But they work best when the second Rule of Attraction is internalized: the problem is more important than the solution.

Communication Breakdown

Here's a weighty, weighty truth: Customers do not care about the benefits and solutions offered by our companies. I know, it hurts to hear it, but it's true.

Far too often marketers make broad, sweeping assumptions when communicating their message to clients. This happens in both the selling interaction (face-to-face and on the phone) as well as the marketing interaction (with ads, brochures, Web sites.) The tendency is a natural one: as marketers, we know far more about our products and services than our customers do, and in fact, we know far more about our customers, too! In many cases, we may know what the customer needs more than they themselves know. There's a danger in that knowledge, though, as it leads to our addressing an ideal audience instead of a real one. The real audience, made up of actual people leading actual lives, cares neither about our benefits nor our solutions. Not one bit.

I know. It doesn't hurt less to hear it a second time.

I've said this publicly and been stared down as crazy. Traditional sales and marketing methods teach that we should elaborate on our features and benefits, so that prospects will see how they can be helped by our solutions, and thus will logically decide to buy, invest, attend.

Yet this assumption is the rotten root of crumbling sales and failed marketing. It's flawed from its foundations.

Individuals today make buying decisions based on emotion more than logic. Thus, it's quite useless to assume that one's audience will be following the logic lined out for them in our demographic notes. If it's emotion that sells, then we must learn to care about what our customers care about. In this case, our prospects care far, far more about their problems than they will ever care about our remarkable solutions.

I believe that *nothing* Morgan could have shown the fast food execs would have convinced them to make any sort of change. Nothing would have convinced them. Not until some pain was inflicted. There is no change without pain.

By speaking to our prospects and customers in terms of their problems, we help them feel comfortable with us; like former President Clinton, we have felt their pain. But we've also appealed not to their logic but to their emotions. They're attracted to us already, and we've never even given them a pitch. By the time you begin to share what you're offering, the deal is already done.

Basic anatomy tells us—sorry, we're back in high school again—that the brain is divided into two parts: the right and left hemispheres. For this reason, it is common for someone to describe himself or herself as being "left-brain" oriented, meaning he or she is more logical, precise, and analytical. Conversely, those with high right-brain function are more emotional, creative, and feeling-oriented. When we talk about problems, we tend to stimulate the right side of the brain, thus activating the emotions. When we talk about solutions, we tend to activate the left side of the brain, where people analyze our solutions and logically determine if our solution actually fits their specific needs or solve their problems.

What anatomists have taught, however, has major application here: *it's easier for someone to process information that is addressed to the right brain.* And it's more pleasant for most people (Einstein excluded, of course) to process right brain oriented information—creative, feeling and image oriented data. This is why most advertising tends to stimulate emotions and speaks in pictures. And this is why television is such a powerful medium: it communicates in moving images and sounds which provoke strong feelings like sadness, happiness, arousal, or disgust. You hardly ever hear someone say, "I think I'll go home tonight and look at some spreadsheets or do a little calculus." Excluding physicists and math teachers, most average folks flip on the tube and let the gamma rays wash over them. It's more than simple laziness: those images and emotions stimulate one's right brain for a few hours. If we can speak in terms of the problem, we'll be just as attractive. We'll activate emotions, foster longing, and help our audience remember and care about what we're offering.

How to Find the Problem: A Four-Step Solution

Marketers like to believe they each have a unique solution, and many are confident they are different from the competition. Ironically, however, when comparing marketing strategies, they all end up sounding the same, focusing on what the company, product, or service *does*. The language promises a generic group of benefits in which buyers *may* be interested. Even the best marketing materials (Web sites, brochure, flyers, ads, radio or TV spots, promotions, interactive CDs or videos) attempt to communicate to the customer why a particular product is better than the competition. Few focus on the problems that the customer is having. Few address the emotional elements. Few powerfully activate the right hemisphere of the brain. Thus, few are taking advantage of the attraction mindset.

So how do we focus on the problem, instead of on the solution? Herewith, the four-step process.

Step One: Problem Identification

Identify the major problems that your prospects and customers may be facing. Discover how living with this problem affects them. How does it make them feel? What does it prevent them from doing? How could things be better for them if the problem were to evaporate? In short, what pain is this problem causing the customer or prospect?

Sounds simple. But this step, the most important, may be more difficult than you think. You must be sure that when you do identify the problem, it really *is* the problem.

In the 80s, Burger King made a ruinous marketing blunder. They determined that the "problem" which fast-food consumers had encountered was the difficulty in finding good-tasting fast food. With this as their starting point, they concluded that since "flame-broiled" hamburgers tasted better, stressing this feature of their burgers in their marketing would win them more customers. Consequently, they created a marketing campaign that focused on "flame-broiled" burgers as their exclusive solution to the customers' problem.

But they had one problem: they had misidentified the problem.

The real problem that confronted consumers—and therefore their motivation in choosing a particular company over another—was not the need for a tasty meal; rather, it was the need for a cheap, and convenient meal that one could have customized to his or her specific preference. I don't have to tell you that the "flame-broiled" marketing plan went up in smoke. But the campaign that followed was spot on: "Have it your way." This exclusive claim—that Burger King could offer food that was cheap, convenient, and customized—was far more effective. At the time, BK was the *only* fast food restaurant to offer freedom of choice. For their efforts they nearly overtook the number one position in the fast food industry held by McDonalds. Problem identified. Problem addressed. Customers attracted.

Step Two: Remove Yourself from the Solution

This step is the one most often overlooked—probably because it is so counterintuitive. Once a target audience is identified, many become so anxious to get the business that they scare the customer away. As I said in the Introduction, if the lion pride knew the Rules of Attraction, they'd recline beneath Eucalyptus trees and act disinterested until the gazelle wandered by, feeling falsely secure. But like lions, we act on instinct: we identify the problem and we immediately move to the solution. And we spend far too much energy bounding across the plain in search of a customer that is more afraid than attracted.

It is for this reason that most marketing is ineffective. Web sites, brochures, print ads, commercials, even business presentations—when they quickly identify the problem then dedicate the majority of time, space, and priority to "why and how" the marketer solves this problem, they miss the moment of attraction.

Want to hear something better? Try proposing solutions in a way that does not overtly promote your company, product, or service.

Sound ridiculous? Isn't the purpose of marketing to promote your products, get new clients, increase market share, and ultimately sell more? Of course! But that "more" will be far more if it's won by attraction rather than aggression.

I advise that one first promote the "generic" solutions before giving his or her exclusive solutions. Why? First, if you remove yourself from those obvious solutions, you win the chance to align your client's thinking with yours. Both of you stand on the side of the problem, looking out at the landscape of solutions. Second, your approach appears selfless: your proposition is communicated with the best interest of the prospect in mind. Later, when you begin to demonstrate the exclusive solution, the customer begins to realize of his own volition that your solution is simply better than the generic solutions. And in many cases, they'll realize yours might very well be their *only* solution!

This amounts, in a sense, to a strategic comparative marketing approach. Which brings me to the comedic genius of Jerry Seinfeld. Stay with me.

George and Elaine borrow Jerry's car to go to the swap meet. On their way back, George runs over a pothole and the car begins to make a noise. Fearful that Jerry will become angry, the two pseudo-friends hatch a plan. Elaine goes to Jerry and in an excited, animated way she describes how she and George were chased by a pack of wild teenagers in a supped-up vehicle. They chased them at high speeds! They fired a gun in the air! George was even driving the car on two wheels to get away! Jerry hugs her and thanks God that she and George are okay. As an afterthought, she adds that they ran over a bump and the car is making a noise. Jerry's reaction is predictable: "No problem, the important thing is that you are all back safe." Under any other set of circumstances Jerry would have been furious that George and Elaine damaged his car. But the fact that the car is making a noise is of far less importance than the safety of his friends. The comparative illustration deflects Jerry's anger. In the same way a generic solution can be used to deflect the prospect's tendency to resist your company's specific solution. The generic solution must be presented in a believable and comprehensive way that demonstrates one theme: even by applying all of the generic solutions there remains a gap in satisfaction. If that can be proven to the customer, your exclusive solution will sound incredibly powerful.

Step Three: Suggest an Exclusive Solution

For years marketers have learned the way to differentiate their company, product or service was to create a USP (Unique Selling Proposition). Ready for another bombshell?

The USP is ineffective.

What is effective? USP's must be replaced by ***Exclusive Solutions***. It's that simple. Solutions must be specifically tailored to solve the customer's problems. Only by fully understanding the customer's problem can we design the exclusive solutions. Ask yourself these questions: What do you do that is so different from your competitors that it makes you the *only* solution to the problems you've identified? How can you use this knowledge to develop marketing language that speaks emotionally and references the problems that you have identified? How can you do this in an emotionally-charged way that stimulates the right hemisphere of their brain?

Theodore Vail was one of the most effective developers of the exclusive solution in history. The president of Bell Systems at the turn of the century, Vail built the company into what was to become the largest private business in the world. So large was Bell that the government had to break it up into many smaller companies—and it was such a behemoth that it took nearly an entire decade to accomplish the break-up of the monopoly.

Back in 1914, however, Bell was in big trouble. Its phone patents had expired and other smaller companies were getting into the business.

Suddenly, Bell had competition. What was once an exclusive solution was now about to become very generic indeed. Vail solved this problem in three ways. First, he decided Bell would be called AT&T (American Telephone and Telegraph). Because in that day not many American citizens had experience using a telephone but they all were comfortable with sending a telegraph. Vail created a name that customers could see as emotionally safe for them. He also decided that the company would build the most reliable phone system in the world, and this at a time when the phone service was anything *but* reliable. In a time when service could often be suspended for hours or even days, a commitment to reliability was truly an exclusive claim.

Next, he committed the company to building a long-distance system that would cross the entire United States. To do this, he knew he would have to invest in scientific research, and so he developed AT&T's own research laboratory, Bell Labs. He agreed to cooperate with competitors, leasing them the use of AT&T's phone lines. He also managed to convince the public and the government that the best possible phone system was one that could provide "universal service" around the country; in essence, the best phone system would come from a monopoly like AT&T. As a result of this exclusive solution, AT&T became the *only* player in a huge industry.

Step Four: Test Risk Reversal

When clients entertain making a change, as in a supplier or vendor change, there is an inherent risk of which they are keenly aware. As they say, the grass isn't always greener on the other side, and even if it is, the friction to get over there is painful. Therefore, it is important that we help clients to see that by taking our advice we are actually reversing that risk. There are a number of ways to do this. You can use guarantees, promises, or even offer their money back based on performance. Or you can demonstrate proof that your exclusive solution actually works. Once you have shown a prospect that you understand their problem, remove yourself from the solution, explore exclusive solutions, and show that there is little to no risk in using your solution, your evidence will build credibility for all of the claims you've made. You can use client testimonials, industry examples, dramatic demonstrations—any form of evidence you can to back up all of your claims.

Whether you are talking to prospects in the selling role or preparing marketing material that will be used to create attraction, I encourage you to go out and find some problems that your prospects are facing. Focus on these problems when you prepare your message. Look for ways to emotionally communicate the problems. Talk about what could happen if the problem continues. Finally, propose an exclusive solution and reverse their risk in changing. This technique allows us to become far more attractive than the typical benefit-oriented solution.

Personal Action Plan:

- What are the most difficult problems for your prospects and customers?
- How does it make them feel? What does it prevent them from doing?
- How could things be better for them if they DIDN'T have this problem?
- What PAIN is this causing the customer or prospect?
- What are some of the things that you can do or say that would allow the customer to perceive that you are actually removing yourself or your company from their solution?
- What do you do that is so different from your competitors that it makes you the ONLY solution to the problems you've identified?
- How can you use this knowledge to develop marketing language that emotionally speaks in terms of the problems that you have identified?
- How can you do this in an emotionally charged way that stimulates the right hemisphere of their brain?
- What can you do that will reverse your clients risk in changing?

Rule #3:

Create an Exclusive Community of Super-users

Passion

Want to get a reaction out of somebody? Say two words.

Mel Gibson.

Controversy has surrounded the actor over the past half decade, and no one is without an opinion. The man we once thought was just another Hollywood package has become anything but "just another." He broke from the pack, partly due to a movie that changed his image in a matter of days. And he wasn't even in it!

Gibson's *The Passion of the Christ* opened in more than 3,000 theaters, an unusually large release for any movie. But this one was a religious film. In which the actors spoke dead languages. And the audience read subtitles. The plot was sparse. It was politically incorrect—Christians are less popular today than the gay community. It was filled with more blood, gore, and torture than Wes Craven and Tim Burton could ever have imagined. Yet advance ticket sales hit $10 million, and the first weekend generated over $100 million in sales. Gratuitous violence, no dialogue, little character development, no advertising, and not a recognizable actor on the screen or in the credits—how did Gibson ever sell this film? How could a movie that depicts the final twelve hours of the life of Jesus Christ, in excruciating detail, end up being an historic success? Eschewing the Hollywood formula for successful filmmaking, *The Passion of The Christ* was the first religious film that actually ended up being a blockbuster.

Newsweek said of the film, "When all is said and done, he's made what may be the most watched passion play of all time. Putting his money where his mouth was, Gibson invested $20 million of his own cash in a film so divisive that no Hollywood studio would touch it."

Regardless of one's religious beliefs, one fact is not in question: Mr. Gibson was passionate—*obsessive*—about telling this story. He did what he loved and he did it with enthusiasm. With the standards of his industry and his culture against him, he created something exceptional, new, interesting, compelling—something worth noticing and worth talking about. And he built the marketing right into the product itself.

Hmmmm.

If we create something virus-worthy then figure out how to sneeze it onto as many people as possible, we may well inspire a revolution. Tom Peters says in his book *The Pursuit of Wow* that the only products or services that will succeed in the future will be those that are created by passionate people. Gibson used the hive mentality to create sneezers (the Christian community) to develop something virus-worthy. He didn't create an ad campaign that catered to the masses. That would have been trying to swim upstream. Instead, he went with the flow: Gibson previewed the movie to evangelical media and church leaders.

Focusing on this small, self-contained hive market was very smart marketing indeed. Evangelicals were the market segment most influential, most profitable, and most likely to sneeze. And sneeze they did—all over each other. Through radio stations, television networks, publications, and Web sites, this religious community was *infected*.

Not long after the marketing had begun, churches across the country reserved entire theaters for the opening. According to *People* magazine, "The National Association of Evangelicals, which represents more than 50 denominations and 43,000 congregations, even helped sell tickets on their Web sites. The religious community embraced the film as 'the best outreach opportunity in 2,000 years,' according to the Rev. Rob Schenck, President of the National Clergy Council. Pope John Paul II seeing the movie said, 'It is as it was.' Billy Graham was so moved that he wept and called it a film equal to a lifetime of sermons."

Gibson started with ***passion***, and engaged the strategy of ***infection*** to win greater share of heart. Small business owners should be as inspired as the religious communities that flocked to the film.

Don't for a moment reduce Gibson's work to a profiteering exercise. On the contrary, I believe that the film enjoyed success in part—or primarily—due to his passion and focus. He created an evangelistic tool to spread a message he *believed* in.

The moral?

Kill the profit motive. Aim for the heart.

As we've seen in the previous Rule, clearly understanding the challenges and problems of those in our selected target audience helps us to become more important to and gave influence with them. It logically follows that the target audience we select will be one for which we possess empathy and affinity. And it's likely the solutions we develop for this audience will relate to a subgroup that we know, understand, even *love*.

When that happens, who needs advertising?

Advertising Sucks

Launching successful products without traditional advertising or promotion—it's happening everywhere we turn.

As a fledgling Marketing Manager with Walker International, a top consulting firm, I was delivering my first major presentation to the board of directors, when the CEO bellowed in my direction, "It's a HOPE business, son. You HOPE someone sees your ad, you HOPE they call you, and then you HOPE they buy something."

Cocky New Jersey Italian that I was (ur…*am*), I swallowed hard and moved ahead, prepared to wax eloquent and persuasively on my topic: why our company should start advertising. A 28-year-old junior executive in a billion dollar conglomerate, I took on the CEO, and aimed to do battle with one of his long-held principles: absolutely no advertising.

I lost.

But I learned something valuable from the battle: traditional advertising rarely works. In fact, the more non-traditional the marketing, the more dramatic the response (read: Mel Gibson).

We've talked about *attraction* as an alternative to *aggression* in chasing down prospects. It's the first intangible in winning *heartshare*. But go one step further—what if we could create a form of attraction that also *infects*! (Now that gives me goose bumps!)

I was in a daze for a half a day after reading the article in *Fast Company* magazine—(Note to non-subscribers: your life is incomplete. *Fast Company* is the coolest business publication on the planet. Check it out: www.fastcompany.com)—about buzz marketing. Because this kind of buzz marketing was unlike anything I'd ever seen.

Creating "Buzz Agents"

Linda Tischler described a consulting firm that companies hire for one purpose: to create buzz for their products or services. An entire company dedicated to *attraction* and *infection*. The company is called *BzzAgents* and they sell only one product: **Buzz**. When a client signs on, *BzzAgents* searches its database for agents that match the demographic and psychological profile of their target customer. They then contract with these thousands of "agents" to spread the gospel, as it were. Agents receive information about the client as well as free samples. They have very specific goals in terms of creating positive propaganda and get this: *they are not paid a dime!* They do the work because they actually believe in the product or service they are representing.

Don't think you're going to rush out and hire *BzzAgents*. First, BzzAgents rejects eighty percent of the companies that try to hire them. I had their founder, David Butter on my radio show and he said plainly, "We can help a product that has value but we just can't help a product that's schlock" (his words folks, not mine!). On top of that, the average twelve-week campaign typically deploys more than 1000 agents and carries a hefty price tag–close to $100,000. Recent clients include Anheuser Bush, Monster.com and Land's End.

Worry not. You don't need to sell your firstborn to create infectious buzz and bump your share of heart. You can do it on your own in just a few months with a well-crafted buzz marketing campaign and a few well-chosen representatives. How?

First, you have to have something good to say, and a unique story with which to say it. Then start only with a handful of loyalists. Give them something special: something valuable, in demand, and limited in supply. Finally, work at educating and inspiring them. Turn them into evangelists. Not for the sake of profit, but for their own edification. Then get out of the way and listen.

Bzzzzzzz.

What's that sound? It's somebody talking about your company.

A World Now Connected by Super-Users

If I were Steve Jobs, I'd be mad.

He invents the personal computer and IBM steals his idea, perfects it, and starts a revolution that has now been passed on to Michael Dell, Ted Waitt, et al.

Then Jobs developed his GUI (graphical user interface), otherwise known as the mouse, and his pal Bill Gates swipes that.

Still undeterred, Jobs and his super-geeks come up with a way to link computers using a sophisticated new technology called Earthnet. Their vision: every computer in the world could communicate with every other computer for the purposes of sharing information. Xerox told him he was out of his mind. Who would want to share that much information? After all, the world was full of competitors trying to keep as much information out of the other guy's hands as possible.

So Earthnet became the Internet. It just took a while.

And now Apple has created a new series of personal gadgets that have redefined the role of technology in everyday life.

Do you think we'd better sit-up and listen?

I've learned to stop being surprised by Apple innovation: I wouldn't be surprised if the mouse and the keyboard became obsolete and we began communicating by sending instant real-time audio clips to our super-user networks. But that's another book.

Here's what's most amazing about Apple: They have developed several groups of super-users that are still so dedicated to the Apple platform that they refuse to even acknowledge the limitations of the product. Apple has leveraged several of the rules of attraction to their benefit. While the number of Apple machines is miniscule when compared to the PC/Windows compatible machines, they tend to command almost a cult following. Look at the educational market, the advertising business, and the graphic design industry. All are *dominated* by Apple and Mac machines. Why? Because they are customized to be more ergonomic, efficient, and intuitive for those specific applications. Apple may never *rule* the world but they will continue to create ground-breaking innovations that will *change* the world. And they will launch them and popularize them through their ruthlessly loyal super-user network.

And that's why Steve Jobs is happy.

Hogwarts or Hogwash?

After the fourth hour of standing on line, my niece finally held the final *Harry Potter* book in her hands. The eagerness on her face was the ultimate signifier of childhood joy and, yes, terribly effective marketing.

The publisher of the *Harry Potter* series, Scholastic Publishing, has earned over $600 million on book sales alone from the brand. The first print run for the seventh book was more than ten million copies—more than any single book run in history. And it sold out in under 24 hours! According to the European news agency Reuters, all ten million copies of the book had to kept under lock and key at retailers worldwide for fear of customer rioting. Security was so high they even delivered the books to local retailers by a fleet of armored cars. If that's not enough, the movies and DVDs have earned more than $3 billion, and the numbers will only continue to climb.

What happened? How? Through the honesty, innocence, and wonder of her stories, Rowling created a network of super users, all of them as fiercely loyal to Harry and his small band of friends.

Suicide by Marketing

This is going to sound dramatic, so be prepared.

Traditional sales and marketing is suicide in today's business environment.

Why? Because traditional media isn't only less effective, it actually pushes more customers away than it attracts. That's right: traditional methods tend to alienate target customers.

Two numbers to surprise you:

A recent McKinsey & Company study revealed about traditional TV advertising: "TV advertising expenditures will be only **one-third as effective** in 2010 as they were in 1990."

Briggs and Stuart, in their new book *What Sticks: Why Most Advertising Fails* assert that **thirty-seven percent of all advertising is wasted**.

Those are amazing statistics. And they reveal how the world of marketing has gone through a radical evolution—and that most are still unaware of this. So many businesses are still pouring millions of dollars into ineffective forms of marketing that has little or no chance of succeeding.

A New World

This is not an overstatement: every form of traditional media is in crisis. Radio stations, TV networks, newspapers, and magazines are suffering from a *double-digit drop* in business. They are lamenting the glory days of advertising when marketers waited on line, cash in hand, for a premium ad position in order to tout their message. It was a volume game. The more you advertised, the more you sold.

That was the old world.

This is the new.

Customers today—with more choices than ever, and far less time to make those choices—*ignore* most traditional advertising. Thus, standard forms of marketing have been rendered effectively *invisible*. Instead, they listen to their friends, associates, and the more "alternative" forms of media.

So imagine spending thousands or even millions of dollars on radio, TV, outdoor or print advertising, only to discover that you hadn't gained even one additional customer from that expense. That's enough to ruin your day—or your career.

Welcome to the New World, where viral marketing holds the power. The most successful marketers are adept at creating a buzz. They find the super-users and align themselves with influencers or *sneezers*. Then they inoculate the sneezers with their message or buzz and watch the word spread.

But buzz is a tricky magic to master. It must, above all, be pure and honest, rather than sales-y and promiscuous. And it must be spread in a smooth, persistent way so it is amplified into Gladwell's eventual Tipping Point. This is the point where every person in your target audience simply *must have* your product or service—like the iPod in everybody's pocket or UGG Boots on everybody's feet.

Just as there was a formula for the successful direct marketing of the past, there is also a formula for creating a "buzz virus."

AUDIO CONTENT: "NO MORE SUICIDE"

I have created a 10 minute audio file on this topic.

I have sent this audio segment to hundreds of entrepreneurs and I am amazed the results they have produced. To request this audio file go to www.markdeo.com. Here's my action plan for putting the super-user network philosophy to work for your business:

Personal Action Plan

- Identify the smallest most influential market that you can possibly find - a powerful, yet reputable subgroup that will have interest in what you have to offer.
- Create a premium product or service that is so impressive and compelling and offer it ONLY to this group.
- Figure out a way to give them a small taste of the product. Do so in advance of everyone else.
- Empower the leaders of this group to make claims and statements to their community regarding the product that you have created.
- Build your marketing right into your product or service rather than tagging it on as an afterthought.

Rule #4:

Become the Only Solution

A Question of Positioning

Don't you miss monopolies? With a monopoly you don't have to worry about marketing or advertising because you don't have to worry about competition. Monopolies *demand* attraction (though of a false, obligatory kind). But all that pesky government reform took care of monopolies forever and ruined all the easy fun. Now we must rely on positioning our solution in a favorable way so that we *create* attraction. ***Positioning*** is the process of defining your business solution in the clearest of terms. It encapsulates precisely how your solution to the customer's problem eliminates their pain and adds value. It also outlines a strategy to set you apart from the competition.

Take a look at some of the questions "positioning" answers:

- How does your product or service uniquely suit the needs of your target audience?
- What specific benefits can your prospects expect?
- What is your unique competitive advantage?
- What is your business identity?
- What is the reputation of your company?
- How will you package your solution?

The Exclusive Marketing Position

As we discussed in the previous chapter, a business's reputation is often wrapped up in what advertising guru Bill Bernbach called the "Unique Selling Proposition" (USP). What sets you apart from the crowd? What do you do that no one else does? Bernbach suggested this is far more important than the quality or price of your product or service. As I said previously, to make this concept fit into today's buyer and economic needs we need to slightly modify this.

It's important for our marketing position to be more than unique. It must be ***exclusive***: we must *exclusively* solve the problems identified within the target audience that we defined in the previous section. And it must employ *facts*, not *claims*. While making claims of performance may have worked in Bernbach's day, we're forced to employ a different kind of rhetoric today. 40 years ago there were only one or two competitors for every product or service sold. Now there are thousands! Thus, we must move from unique to *exclusive*, from suggestions to *absolutes*, from the "Unique Selling Proposition" (USP) to the "Exclusive Marketing Position" (ESP). We must isolate our exclusive solution to a given problem and support it with evidence that proves we are not the best option but the only solution.

Got Milk?

Milk is a unique commodity. There are no national brands. The only advertising is by industry cooperatives. And local brands are pretty much interchangeable. So why is it that my friend Matt Walker drives seven miles to a dairy in Montebello to buy milk at a price significantly higher than what he can find around the corner from his home? Counting grocery stores, gas stations, liquor stores, and convenience stores, he passes literally dozens of places that sell milk—and all of them sell it cheaper than his chosen vendor. But Matt never hesitates. Why?

Glass bottles.

Broguiere's Dairy, a family owned business since the 1920s, has succeeded in creating a brand name in an industry that's resisted branding, for a product that is handled by more competitors than one can count. How? By selling milk in a glass bottle. Is the milk from a glass bottle any different, any better? Nope. But Broguiere's has discovered that their customers have found something satisfying in buying milk packaged similarly to the way it was for their grandfathers. The glass bottle does seem to be colder than the plastic containers, and it has a pleasing firmness to the dented and yellow plastic jugs one finds behind the glass door freezer of the convenience store. Because of this unique packaging, Broguiere's bottles have become collector's items, with special limited edition versions being swapped on eBay. Their glass bottles are distributed in high-end grocery stores such as Bristol Farms. And since customers have their bottles, when they bring them back to the dairy or the store, they are in a perfect position to become repeat customers.

Matt likes the milk and the container, and buying from Broguiere's makes him feel something—a uniqueness. The milk is fine to me, but what I love about Broguiere's is that they are the *only* solution in terms of milk in a glass bottle—at least in my area of the country. They are setting themselves apart from the crowded marketplace in a major way. Simple exclusivity.

Developing Your Brand

This type of exclusive branding can be accomplished for service-based businesses as well as hard-good products. Let's look at another example, perhaps my favorite: mine. In 1997, I was honored to be asked to host a radio show that aired on the CBS network through Infinity Broadcasting. It was called The Small Business Hour. We were fortunate to be on the air for over ten years and were able to develop a distinctive brand for the show and it was the model for many business talk shows that followed. In this way we were able to develop a powerful brand for something as intangible as a radio show. What did my radio show offer to advertisers that no one else could claim? We had the only radio show in Southern California dedicated to small business improvement. How did this help our clients, the sponsors and advertisers? The benefits were many, and we demonstrated them with incontrovertible evidence!

For example:

- Industry leaders sponsor the show: Farmers and Merchants Bank, Gevity HR, CNM Telecom, iPower and Prepaid Legal. Thus, there is a history of sponsor success.
- With over 20,000 weekly listeners, enough people were listening to constitute a substantial audience.
- The show was Arbitron rated, so you could be confident the stated listener base was *real*, not inflated.
- The average income per listener was more than $95,000 per year, so you knew they had the *capacity* to buy your product or service.

- More than eighty-six percent of our listeners were entrepreneurs or managers in small businesses, so you knew they had a *need* for your product or service.
- The show aired on KLSX 97.1FM, one of the most powerful, well-established stations in Los Angeles at the time, so you knew the listeners will be loyal to the station and show.
- Sponsors were listed in the resources section of smallbusinesshour.com, which had over 300 pages of free valuable information for the small business owner, making it easy to find advertisers.
- For over ten years I hosted the show nearly every single week, making it one of the longest running, most consistently aired talk shows in Southern California, so on-air recommendations had a great deal of credibility.
- The show aired on the CBS radio network, one of the largest and most respected networks in the country, so there was a high visibility for everyone involved with the show on other CBS stations.
- Sponsors participated in our "Weekly Business Update" that was sent to over 2000 opt-in subscribers every week, so you had an opportunity to educate those listeners most loyal to our network.
- We were named Small Business Journalists of the Year for 2003 by the Small Business Administration, proving that our show was taken seriously by our audience and the industry.
- We held Small Business seminars and classes in marketing and management for entrepreneurs and small business owners to help forge a personal connection with listeners and sponsors.

This was the solid evidence of exclusive marketing position, and we consistently communicated it in every media message we employed—on our Website, in our brochure, on our business cards, and in conversations.

Creating Exclusivity for Your Business

Enough with the Mark Deo commercial.

The purpose of my yammering on about *my* radio show is merely to demonstrate how *you* can develop your own exclusive marketing position.

How are you different? What makes you exclusive to your target audience? What do you do to support that exclusivity? How can you consistently communicate that in your marketing message?

The more precise and exclusive your message, the more powerful it will be to your target audience. You can't be everything to everybody. Set yourself apart for a small select group. This will shield you against most competitors and make you more valuable to your best type of prospects.

Let's take a closer look at this exclusive marketing position as it applies to your business. Consider the following:

What makes your company different? What do you offer that NO ONE ELSE does? What is different about your target audience? Remember that your Exclusive Marketing Position is more about the position your company, product, or service occupies in the marketplace than what you memorize and say. While these facts about your business will be articulated, the important thing to get is that they define your market position.

Exclusive Marketing Position (EMP) Worksheet

List five things that your company does differently than your competition:

1)

2)

3)

4)

5)

List five exclusive attributes about your core product or service:

1)

2)

3)

4)

5)

What pain do they alleviate for your customers?

What specific problems do they solve?

What specific solutions do you provide for this exclusive audience? What specific benefits does your product/service uniquely provide for them?

Breakthrough Innovation

Attraction happens naturally when you create a product so innovative that it becomes an exclusive solution by its very nature. Kleenex. Microsoft Windows. The most dramatic innovation transforms processes to create superior customer satisfaction, rather than simply product improvement.

Innovation is no longer an optional advantage; it is a mandatory objective for all businesses. Its benefits are numerous, and it helps with market and mind share. But more than that, true innovation creates attraction, and allows us to capture heartshare.

Innovation:

- Increases market share by overstepping the competition.
- Increases mind share by making our products and services more memorable and attractive.
- Increases heartshare by achieving greater efficiency and a smoother customer experience.

Levels of Innovation

We innovate at one of four levels: Standard, Specialized, Extraordinary and Breakthrough. I have no category for the non-innovator, because I believe each business has the ability to move forward consistently and powerfully. A zero level of innovation reflects not the potential of a company, but the level at which that company has been able to follow the rules of attraction, which generate innovation naturally.

Standard Innovation

This first level of innovation merely allows us to keep pace with the changes in our industry. It could also be called *survival innovation*. At this level, companies innovate their products and services only enough to minimize the gap between themselves and the industry leaders. Engaging in this kind of reactive innovation, rather than proactive innovation, means organizations are relying on the competition's initiatives. As such, standard innovation, or survival innovation, will inevitably lead to stasis. It's this level at which most small businesses are functioning.

Specialized Innovation

This second level of innovation typically occurs when an organization adapts their product or service to a specific marketplace or subgroup. While in the consumer electronics business, I consulted for a company named Bogen, a manufacturer of public address systems. When this market went south, the company saved themselves from extinction by directing all of the internal elements of their business to the marine marketplace. A small but virtually untapped subgroup, the shift was profitable, and the production, technical, and service innovations were relatively minor to accomplish this. Bogen quickly captured nearly one hundred percent market share and mind share among the marine subgroup. More importantly, by paying attention to previously overlooked dealers and distributors, they snagged a good deal of heartshare too.

Extraordinary Innovation

At this level of innovation—which, as its name suggests, is not typical—organizations leverage their uniqueness to deliver a level of otherness that their competitors are not currently offering. Case in point: the astounding innovation built into the production and service guarantee of Pelican Products. Their claim: "You break it. We replace it. *Forever*." This phrase is far different than marketing hype, as the company manufactures carrying cases and flashlights that are virtually indestructible. The product is sold to the military, law enforcement, fire and emergency agencies. Their remarkable guarantee is unmatched in their industry and their competitors are stymied by their ability to continue to offer this year after year. Even more amazing, Pelican tells me their return rate is less than one percent. How do they do this? By coupling the guarantee and the product and thus giving customers an exclusive innovation. How big is the market for industrial cases and flashlights? The company will do almost $100 million this year. It helps to have massive heartshare.

Breakthrough Innovation
Breakthrough innovation occurs when an organization makes a revolutionary advancement in one or more of the innovation processes. In this case, a company will deliver a level of innovation that their competitors are *not capable* of offering. Many times these organizations literally create monopolies that admittedly have a half-life—yet they permit them to rapidly capture huge market, mind, and heartshare almost instantly. Read: Microsoft. This is where innovation meets the exclusivity: the level of innovation achieved is clearly evidenced by the creation of an exclusive solution. These companies become not just a better solution but the *only* solution.

As you can see, innovation isn't always about changing the product or service itself. Innovation can and should occur in several different areas of business development. We can create innovation in processes as well. Many organizations have gained market advantage by innovating internal variables such as their production process, delivery, technical support, or customer service elements.

Internal Innovation

In order to create a world class product, service, or company we must integrate innovation into many areas of our business—internal as well as external elements. Internal elements would be the processes inside the business such as manufacturing or production, delivery of products or services, administration and accounting systems. These internal innovation variables are separate of the external elements such as sales, marketing or branding. The chart on the next page shows how we can evaluate our innovation position for each area and plan for continued internal or external innovation. Go to www.markdeo.com/rulesofattraction to complete this form and submit it for our evaluation.

Innovation Continuum

Plot your company's position for each of the six processes on the Innovation Continuum. Then write in each of the boxes what a standard, specialized, extraordinary and breakthrough innovation would look like for each of the six processes. Go to www.markdeo.com/rulesexercises.htm to complete this form and submit it for our evaluation.

	Internal Variables			External Variables		
	Production	Delivery	Service	Sales	Marketing	Branding
Breakthrough						
Extraordinary						
Specialized						
Standard						

External Innovation

External innovation includes building improvement into the selling process, the branding strategy, or the marketing approach. Look at how retailers like Home Depot, Wal-Mart, Ikea, and Amazon have innovated the shopping process. The latest releases and the major brands priced with razor thin margins, all in one place, with near instant gratification. Because of the competitive nature of nearly every product or service category today, innovation is often a very effective force when applied to the areas of marketing and branding. Harley Davidson has innovated the image of the "biker." Now bikers wearing denim and leather are more likely to be Federal Circuit Court Judges and brain surgeons than the wild hoodlums of just two decades ago.

Many in price-sensitive, commodity-oriented industries are persuaded that this kind of innovation won't work for them. While there may be very few commodity-oriented businesses where innovation is impossible or unnecessary, every business can innovate to some degree. Think of the lowly paperclip. How innovative can you get with paper clips? Been to the office supply store lately? It's an entertaining stroll. Colored paper clips, stripped paper clips, day-glow paper clips, alternatively shaped paper clips, magnetic paper clips and so on. Innovation applies to *all* industries and business categories. To remind yourself, go buy a pack of tie-dyed paperclips.

To demonstrate the expansive application of innovative practice, consider the monopoly and bureaucracy. You might not expect innovation from government agencies like the IRS or the Postal Service. But have you called the IRS lately? On the other end of the phone is a person—one that's rather knowledgeable, courteous, and helpful. I was so shocked, I did enough digging to figure it out: the IRS is in the midst of a massive innovation program. And how about that institution of snail mail – the US Post Office? Their Web site evinces a level of attention has gone into branding, communication, and customer service. Folks like FedEx and UPS have forced the Postal System to innovate for the sake of survival. If your mailman is pushing the envelope and bureaucrats are innovating, it's time you did too!

It helps to remember that innovation and invention are very different forces, and we're speaking in terms of economics rather than technology. One needn't apply for patents to foster an ethic of innovation within his or her business. As Webster's will tell you, innovation is "a new device or process created by study and experimentation." It's illuminating to remember that "experimentation" is a core part of the process of innovation. Innovation comes with effort: in short, try.

Peter Drucker, in *The Essential Drucker*, says, "The most productive innovation is a different product or service creating the new potential of satisfaction, rather than an improvement." He goes on to conclude, "In the organization of the business enterprise, innovation can no more be considered a separate function than marketing. It is not confined to engineering or research but extends across all parts of the business, all functions, all activities. Innovation is ultimately the task of endowing human and material resources with new and greater wealth." Drucker obviously understood the concept of heartshare back in 2001 when his book was published. Creating innovation is no longer a luxury, but a pre-requisite.

Memes

It is not just *innovative products* that allow us to become a better option—it's *innovative communication*, speaking and showing the benefits of our products and services in a way that capitalizes on our exclusivity. Have you ever looked at a brochure, Web site, print ad, or mailer, and had to read it twice to figure out exactly what it was all about? Have you ever listened to someone talk about their business only to wonder what kind of product or service they provide? What went wrong in those communications? They failed to find their *meme*.

Marketing memes give us the ability to become instantly understood. The word *meme* is a strange one, to be sure, as it's a concept borrowed from biologist turned social theorist Richard Dawkins. In 1976, the Oxford University professor wrote a book called "The Selfish Gene" in which he introduced the concept of the "meme." Like a gene is the basic unit of biology, passing down traits from person to person, a "meme" is a self-replicating *idea* that is passed along from person to person, making meaning in a culture. He cited examples of memes: memorable tunes, ideas, catch-phrases, fads and so on. Just as genes propagate themselves in the gene pool by leaping from body to body in the form of sperm, memes propagate themselves by leaping from mind to mind in a form of cultural imitation.

A Meme...

- ...is obvious in its meaning
- ...focuses on the outcome
- ...is self-explanatory and simplistic
- ...is easy to replicate in someone's mind
- ...actively transfers information

Developing the Meme

The meme is not necessarily a slogan, headline, or a tag, but it is most effective in that form. Simply put, a meme is your core message; in some ways, it's your branding statement, your identifier, often your logo. Don't have a meme? Make one!

Here's how:

- First ask, "What do my clients get as a result of using my service?"
- Next, strip that phrase down to the essentials.
- Try to strike an emotional chord with your meme.
- Make it easy to remember.
- Make sure it rolls off the tongue nicely.

Examples of Memes

The meme is not necessarily a slogan, headline, or tag, but it is most effective in that form.

- American Express – "Don't leave home without it."
- Hewlett Packard – "Expanding possibilities"
- Fiji Film – "You can see the future from here"

- United – “Fly the Friendly Skies”
- Service Merchandise – “One Call. Done.”
- In Focus – “Project yourself”
- Continental – “Work hard. Fly Right”
- Best Buy – “Now that’s a great idea”
- Jeep – “There’s only one”
- Alamo – “Drive Happy”
- AAA – “We’re always with you”
- Moore Paints – “We make it simple. You make it beautiful.”
- Energizer – The Energizer Bunny, “Keeps going and going”

Developing a meme requires a bit of trial and error (read: experimentation is part of innovation!) This is why it is important to test your own meme with those that you are close with. When you communicate your meme, do people ask the right kind of questions?

The meme for my company, SBA Network, Inc. is “Growing your business by creating market advantage.” This prompts the questions, How do you do this? What exactly IS market advantage?

The meme for my weekly radio show, The Small Business Hour, is “Connecting entrepreneurs with the Masters.” This prompts the questions: Who are the masters? How do you connect them with entrepreneurs?

These are precisely the kind of questions that allow me to demonstrate how I am different, how I solve problems, and how I may be the *only* solution in some cases.

Now it’s your turn: happy meme-ing!

Personal Action Plan:

- In what areas of your business are you creating innovation?
- What can you do to expand this effort?
- If you are achieving internal innovation, what can you do to apply innovation to the external functions?

- Plot your company's position for each of the six processes on the Innovation Continuum. Write in each of the boxes what a standard, specialized, extraordinary and breakthrough innovation would be for each of the six processes.
- Complete the Innovation Continuum and review it with your business associates and shareholders. Go to www.markdeo.com/rulesofattraction to complete this form and submit it for our evaluation.
- Get input from clients, prospects and vendors on what you can do to achieve breakthrough innovation in each of the six areas.
- Develop an innovation plan that will give you the ability to create an exclusive solution for each of the areas of performance for you organization.
- Develop your "meme." Tell it to 4 or 5 people. Are they asking the right kind of questions?
- Complete your EMP Worksheet. Go to www.markdeo.com/rulesofattraction to complete this form and submit it for our evaluation.

Rule #5:

Reject Strategically

Just Say No

There's one word that small business owners are always frightened to say to a potential customer: no.

The word *no* could become the most strategic word in your lexicon. The more people you *reject*, the more attractive you become to the discrete market you've identified.

Consider the following question: What is the fastest growing franchise chain in the United States? If you guessed McDonald's, Burger King, or Starbucks, you weren't even close.

Plotting Your Curves

From its humble beginnings barely a decade ago, fitness center Curves International has expanded to nearly 9,000 locations. To put that growth into context, consider that it took McDonald's and Subway twenty-five years to open 6,000 franchise locations. Curves needed just seven.

How could this be? What is the secret of such exponential growth?

The answer is saying no, and saying it as often as necessary.

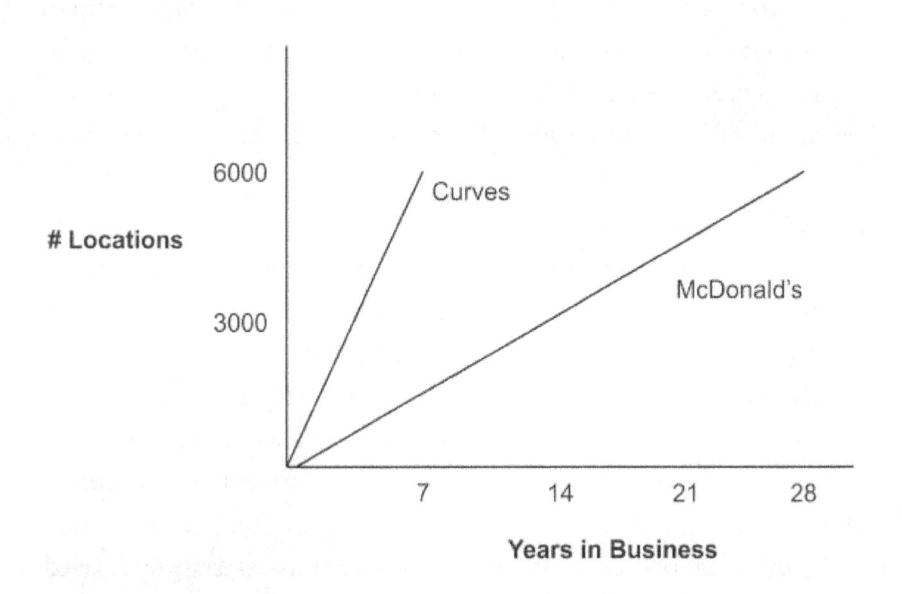

Learning to Love Your No

Bodybuilders are not welcome at Curves. In fact, men in general are few. If you're a casual runner, don't bother showing up. And if you like to walk slowly on a treadmill while watching CNN, this is not the place for you.

Curves targets what has come to be known as "the soccer mom." It was designed to appeal to a female demographic, middle-aged or older, who value expediency, affordability and motivation. Curves is a fitness center, but it differs greatly from other gyms. Instead of 50,000 square feet of saunas, pools, and fancy equipment, a typical Curves franchise occupies 1,200 square feet and holds ten to twelve machines. Simple + Affordable = Moms.

Curves started with Rule number one (become a bigger fish in a smaller pond), and paired it with Rule number five (reject strategically). Together these rules have created breakthrough performance for the company. The lesson is clear, though it sounds odd: when you reject the larger segment of the market, you become more important to your target audience. The result is a product or service that performs exceptionally well when compared with the competition. As right as it feels sometimes, when your continue on the mission to add more business at any cost, regardless of how these new prospects match your target profile, you risk devaluing your market position and reducing your competitive worth.

Not a Numbers Game

I have seen many occasions where management, in pursuit of meeting ever-increasing costs, will do whatever it takes to land a new customer, *any* new customer. Fast forward into the future: if this behavior continues, that company will end up with a great number of new customers and a support nightmare (i.e., too many different versions of a product means support, development and customer services are impossible to maintain). As precious resources are sucked away, the next release of a product or service is constantly delayed. Furthermore, the company may develop a number of features that the market does not want, and the company ceases to be *exclusively important* to anyone. A "jack-of-all-trades" is important to no one. Finally, the profitability for each customer goes down significantly as new features are added only to close deals.

In the long run, businesses die from one of two reasons: (1) having too few customers or (2) having too many of the wrong kind. The more experienced and disciplined strategy is to identify the gap in the marketplace and then develop a solution that fits this need so perfectly that a customer would feel (and be) ridiculous to consider any other inferior solution. This is precisely what companies like Curves are doing. While their centers are incredibly important to the working, mature mother, they are ultimately useless to the average health-enthusiast bodybuilder. And that's just fine.

This strategy does not simply apply to service-based businesses. It works the same way for industrial and consumer products as well.

For example, the Apple iPod is commonly thought to be the hottest consumer electronics product on the market today, but its features ultimately alienate the majority of the marketplace. Think about these limitations: you can't play the iPod unless you use a headphone or attach speakers (it is not self-contained like a radio or boom-box), you can't record with the iPod, if you want to purchase music downloads you must do so through iTunes or a similar site.

The above paragraph translates into only one thing for most buyers: rejection. It's as if Steve Jobs looked deeply into their eyes and said, "It's not for you. It's for me."

If Apple is rejecting so many, why is the iPod performing so well? Instead of broadening its product and begging for the interest of the mainstream, Apple made a product so appealing to its base that the mainstream became converts—by the hundreds of thousands. This is a good example of attraction at work.

Think about your own business. Who's your niche audience? How can you reject the majority of customers and become perfectly customized to that exclusive market who would be idiots not to buy from you and make the rest of the world feel like idiots for not being part of your exclusive market?

Rejected or Rejecter?

The primary definition of *rejection* is "to refuse to accept, submit to, believe, or make use of." As you can see, rejection often relates to ideas about control. Indeed, people who fear rejection often have strange ideas about what they can or should be able to control. When we are rejected, we have lost control, and our first instinct is to seek to regain it. On the other hand, when we reject someone or something, we place ourselves in a position of control, and the response of the person being rejected is to seek acceptance, approval, and affirmation.

Think about it like this: someone has to be rejected, but why does it have to be you? You are either the *rejected*, and thereby out of control, or the *rejecter*, and thereby in control. The trick is to be the first to reject.

Assume you are engaged in a business discussion with a client. Certainly, you intend to persuade or evoke a response from your client or shareholder. The more control you are able to assert into your agenda, the more persuasive you may potentially be. You might ask, "What are some things that I can do to very subtly maintain control over the relationship?" Here are a few examples:

- After some small talk, begin the conversation with a brief overview of the discussion items. In this way, you gain significant control over the conversation. This also allows you to test the waters to discover the primary issues or obstacles.
- Be the one to bring the meeting or phone call to an end. Never wait for the client to bring the meeting to an end. In a sense, you are rejecting further discussion. Always be friendly, never curt or too terse; you are merely the instigator of closure. Often the other party will ask when you will speak again. In this way, you will attract the client to you rather than you having to chase after the client.

Every Conversation Matters

Chances are your customers are not performing at 100 percent of their ability or capacity. If you focus on this part of the relationship rather than on your performance as the vendor, service provider, or supplier, you take the spotlight off of yourself and place it on the customers. When you effectively apply this concept, you are actually acting in the best interest of your customers, setting yourself apart from the competition, and winning a stronger relationship.

Sitting in a client's office several years ago, I recall being asked to help him breathe life back into his sales and marketing efforts. He and his salespeople had been unable to gain and keep the best clients in the industry the way they had in the past. He told me, "We seem to be attracting the bottom of the barrel in the way of clients. I'm referring to the type of clients that don't pay well, consistently demand lower prices, and never seem to be satisfied with our level of service. Maybe it's just our industry. I'm at a loss."

Sound familiar? I told the client that they needed to actually *reject* more clients in order to attract the right ones.

Let's speak concretely: the way a relationship begins usually sets the tone for the entire relationship. If we establish a precedent of being the submissive partner in the relationship then we will always be relegated to the whims of the customer. In Scenario A, below, you're a salesperson making an appointment with a client. Here's a submissive approach:

Scenario A:

CLIENT: Everything sounds fine but I need you to get here at 8 am.

SALESPERSON: Okay, well I'm coming from San Diego but, ummm, I'll try to make it at 8 am.

C: Try? I need a firm commitment on that. Can you make it or not?

SP: Okay, I'll be there. I'll be there at 8.

C: Oh, and I need you to e-mail me an agenda and leave me a voice mail of what you're going to cover.

SP: Sure, fine I can do that. I'll do that tomorrow morning.

C: Why wait until tomorrow? Why can't you do that today? I'm playing golf tomorrow and I really don't want to be bothered while I'm on the course.
SP: Okay, I'll get on it after we hang-up. Anything else?
C: Yeah, let's go to Ruth's Chris Steakhouse for lunch. You've got an expense account right?
SP: Not really—but I'll get a reservation.
C: And one more thing: since you're going to be making a *big* commission on this deal you ought to send me on one of those Ensenada party cruises. That's the least you can do for me getting you this deal.
SP: Alright

Scenario "B" demonstrates how by using rejection in a strategic way we can actually attract the client to doing things our way and happily so:

Scenario B:

C: Everything sounds fine but I need you to get here at 8 am.
SP: Why 8 am?
C: Because that's when I thought we'd start.
SP: I understand but do you mind if I ask you a question first?
C: Sure.
SP: How would it help you to make sure your team is committed to your new solution before we do the meeting?
C: Well, my team would be behind my entire production process change, and that would make me look nice with management.
SP: And that is precisely my goal. So before we start the meeting I'm going to need a couple of things to make that happen. Can you help me?
C: I guess. What do you need?

SP: First, I will need to get a tour of your plant. And I will need to talk to a few salespeople. And then I want some time seeing your current component in application. Can you make that happen?
C: Okay, but I need you to email me an agenda and leave me a voice mail of what you're going to cover.
SP: Don't worry about that. There's no need to waste your time with that kind of stuff right now. Let's define the parameters for the solution so we can position it as a brilliant move on *your* part. I'll be coming from San Diego, so I can't promise to you when I will arrive but it will probably be between 9:30 and 10 am and we'll work all the way through lunch. Can you arrange all that for me when I arrive?
C: Sure. Now, I know you're going to be making a big commission on this deal, so I think you ought to send me on one of those Ensenada party cruises or something. That's the least you can do for me getting you this deal.
SP: What makes you think that I'm making a big commission?
C: Well, aren't you?
SP: No, I am not. But I can restructure the entire deal so that I am and I can get you that trip to Ensenada. However, in that case, I don't think we would even have the budget to do the meeting that you want. Now which is more important to you: a party cruise or getting kudos with management for the right solution?
C: You've got a point there. Alright, I'll get working on the tour and interviews.

This type of approach allows us to control the client, lower their expectations, under-promise and over-deliver. This makes us more attractive and actually builds client loyalty.

The Proposal Follow-up Game

Proposals.

Entrepreneurs and executives often have to create them, and they serve a purpose. But I am often amazed at the level of commitment and time placed into creating proposals with so little guarantee of what that proposal may achieve. It seems that often the creation of the proposal is an act of desperation and hope. Having become so accustomed to jumping when the client asks, often we seem to jump without thinking. We get so excited that the client is actually interested in what we have to offer that we think the deal is " in the bag."

The client says, "Your recommendations sound terrific." That's good. Then the client says, "Can you put together a proposal? Something I can take to my boss, Mr. Sale Stopper?" That's good too. Right? Think again. Why? For a couple of reasons:

First, if you haven't already noticed, customers learn in prospect school that the best way to avoid buying is to procrastinate. When they do this, they are saying neither "no" nor "yes." The result is that they can maintain the relationship with us (the seller), continue to pick our brains (maybe even getting our expertise for free), without making any sort of commitment. This sets the tone for the future relationship. A relationship that is one-sided. A relationship where we have to perform, while they can continue to postpone, delay, and avoid. Even if we do get the business, we can end up working like dogs while they drag their heels with decisions and pay us in their own good time.

Sound familiar?

Second, the proposal request may give them reasons for not doing business with us. Since proposals are not an interactive process, we may inadvertently say the wrong thing and never even know why we lost the sale.

But, you can use rejection to make proposals more attractive. Here's the way I recommend handling the proposal request:

> PROSPECT: Can you put together a proposal for us?
> SELLER: Sure, no problem. May I ask you a question?

PROSPECT: Yes.
SELLER: If we are able to develop a proposal that is acceptable to Mr. Sale Stopper, what would happen next?
PROSPECT: We would do business.
SELLER: Great! If I understand you correctly then, only you and Mr. Sale Stopper are responsible for making the final decision to move forward?
PROSPECT: Correct.
SELLER: Sounds good. Let's review some of the things that we need to put in the proposal to make this happen. You mentioned our weekly service call. What else should we include? What are your key concerns? What are the best solutions? What is most important to Mr. Sale Stopper? Really? Why? What things will be important to you and Mr. Sale Stopper in the future? What would be the main reason Mr. Sale Stopper would not approve the proposal? This is great. Do you think we've developed a winning proposal so far?
PROSPECT: It sounds good.
SELLER: Perhaps I can help you further. Customer service is critical to our firm, and for this reason we have a policy on presenting proposals. Our company requires us to deliver the proposal and present it directly to the buying team. This eliminates any possible confusion, maximizes use of your time and gives you a chance to ask questions. When do you think we may be able to do that with you and Mr. Sale Stopper?
PROSPECT: Well, maybe next Monday at 10am.
SELLER: Great. Now let's look at another scenario. Even with all the elements that we have included in the proposal, it is possible that Mr. Sale Stopper might not go for our proposal. In that event, what would happen next?
PROSPECT: Well, I guess we wouldn't do business.

SELLER: Sounds fair. When would you anticipate making that decision?
PROSPECT: Well, a few days after the proposal, I guess.
SELLER: That sounds reasonable. So if I understand you correctly, Mr. Sale Stopper and yourself will make a final decision on this by Wednesday, at close of business?
PROSPECT: I think we can do that.
SELLER: Great. I'll be working on putting in writing what we've developed today. Can I ask one more thing?
PROSPECT: Sure.
SELLER: Can I call you on Friday to just check in and confirm everything? Perhaps you and Mr. Sale Stopper might think of something else that needs to be added to our proposal?
PROSPECT: Sure.

With this technique, we have significantly increased our chances of developing a winning proposal, as well as lessened the chance of continued procrastination. Most importantly, this is no longer *our* proposal. It is the *client's* proposal. We have strategically secured agreement in advance of putting things in writing. We have created greater value to the proposal on agreeing to a presentation time rather than just mailing or delivering the proposal to the client. And we set a deadline for the approval or denial of the proposal. I will assure you that this technique works nearly every time. It does, however, require practice.

The Ten Absolutes of Rejection

Remember that gaining acceptance often requires practicing rejection. Of course rejection must be practiced with good human relations and with what I like to call heartshare. We will talk more about this when we cover Rule #9. Nevertheless, I have listed below the ***ten absolutes of rejection*** so that you can properly adjust your client/ prospect communication to achieve maximum impact:

1. Conflict is good
2. The customer is NEVER right
3. NEVER make a promise
4. NEVER base new products or services on what you customer says they need
5. NEVER apologize
6. Negotiate EVERYTHING
7. NEVER give anything without getting something back
8. ALWAYS let the customer initiate communication
9. NEVER chase the customer
10. ASK far more questions than you answer

Personal Action Plan

- How can you use rejection to turn away specific segments of the market?
- How can you reject the majority of customers, only to become so perfectly customized to that exclusive market that they would be idiots not to buy from you?
- What business relationships are you engaged in where you feel "controlled?"
- How might you use the concept of strategic rejection to regain control?
- Check your solution against the ten absolutes of rejection. Are you abiding by them in your marketing initiatives and relationships with prospects and clients?

Rule #6:

Give Information Away

Giving it Away

Cameron Diaz, Kate Winslet, Jude Law, Jack Black, Eli Wallach. Not a bad list of A-list movie stars, and also not a bad list of endorsers for your company. My friend and golf buddy Ed Kushins was able to communicate information about his company to the media in such a way that within a few months, these five stars were promoting his company via a major studio motion picture.

Not bad at all.

Kushins is the president of a little company called HomeExchange.com. For a nominal fee, Home Exchange allows homeowners to exchange their homes with others for vacations—and it's all done online with proper security measures. Ed created the company as more of a hobby than anything else, and he used a number of the Rules of Attraction in its formation. Because of the uniqueness of Home Exchange, Ed thought he'd send some media kits to magazines and newspapers to see if they would do a little story on the concept of alternatives to expensive resorts. He focused not on the product or service, but rather on how others were benefiting from their experiences with Home Exchange.

It turned out be an attractive story for magazines, and once a few venues did a story, others followed. Soon, Sony Pictures was beating a path to Ed's door saying they wanted to do a movie about his company. The result? *The Holiday*, a charming film about finding love in unexpected places, with a premise built around HomeExchange.com! Ed now attributes press releases and unpaid articles for much of the growth of his company. To date, he has all but eliminated costly traditional advertising.

The ultimate objective of Public Relations is to get media people to do a story about your business. But first you must get their attention. Since traditional marketing just doesn't work anymore, we must employ street-smart marketing and publicity in order to attract media attention. Here's how Ed prioritizes his PR stories:

About the Company stories
These are usually pretty boring—unless the reader is already interested in what your company has to offer.

New and Improved stories
These are one step better. They tell about some new feature or benefit. Sometimes Ed will create a new feature just so he can announce it. This will usually generate some interest, if only because of the curiosity factor.

Elephant Comes to City Hall stories
These stories are by far the best. Newspapers, magazines, television, and online news sites can't resist showing a picture of an elephant at City Hall. Even if the elephant has nothing to do with your company or product, it will almost surely get you in the paper. Ed suggests that you and your staff find the elephant that will make your story impossible for editors to resist. Be creative, be imaginative, have fun with it. You will get your story out and people will remember you. Here's an example:

> Moving your office to a new town and want to get some press? You probably would not be able to get a cub reporter to return your phone call. But move into your new office and on your first day there present a 6 foot x 2 foot check for $1000 to the local Boys Club. It's our way of saying we are looking forward to being part of this great community, and they will send out a photographer. Much better than a 6 INCH x 2 INCH ad the same $1000 would buy in the same newspaper.

Often the elephant isn't even related with your business. But sometimes it is. Several years ago a television commercial featured men in lab coats standing before

> a table holding national brands of French-fries and ketchup on it. The "researchers" sample the ketchup alone, and conclude that it is good. They then sample a French-fry and conclude it is also good. Then they try the two together, and determine that it is better than either one alone. Instead of a ketchup company going it alone and promoting their product or a French-fry maker buying all the air time themselves, they have combined efforts to present the idea that while their products are good on their own, they are better when eaten together. The whole is far greater than its parts.

This commercial is very effective in that the elephant is someone else's product or service. Never discount the fact that giving free support to another complimentary product or service with yours can actually make your service more attractive and unique. (In the next Rule we will look at alliance and affiliate marketing and how powerful this concept can be in attracting business. Stay tuned!)

Lended Credibility

Instead of viewing other products and services as competitors, look for ways in which you can join efforts to help each other's business. I do a number of seminars every year with the Christopher Howard Companies, and he is a frequent guest on my radio show. Some may say we are competitors: I teach people how to be more successful and so does Chris. So why help out a competitor? Because Chris is more of a *complement* than he is a *competitor*. While we both target the same audience, we teach completely different methods of success. Chris works on the subconscious and I work on the conscious. Working together, we are able to reach a greater market than either one of us could reach independently. In addition, my methods are more powerful when coupled with Chris's technologies; and his are more powerful when coupled with mine. In this way, we actually lend credibility to one another.

You can find collaborators in your industry that lend credibility, and by partnering with them you may be able to create a collective solution that attracts a larger audience than any one element could effectively attract on its own. If you make luggage, find someone that makes luggage carts; if you repair cars, team with car rental services; if you sell musical instruments, find a rehearsal studio bands can use. Simply put: cross promote. And be not afraid of giving away exposure to someone or some product that will end up reflecting back to you. Always be on the lookout for ways in which you can work *with* other entities, rather than ways in which you can *compete* with them. (Again, stay tuned for Rule #10!)

Success on Death Row

While not quite my style of music, Death Row Records is recognized as one of the most successful record companies in history, known strictly for their hardcore rap artists. They have also implemented one of the most brilliant marketing campaigns in the record industry. What they did was incredibly simple and devastatingly effective. And as a result, Death Row has helped launch the careers of completely unknown artists that have since sold hundreds of millions of records.

How did they do this? By giving away information without selling. Included in every established artist's release, Death Row included a song or two featuring a new performer. Some of these "bonus features" highlight just a few seconds of the new artist but in a way that is compelling and evident of their unique style. Without spending a dime on additional marketing, they have given the fans of one performer a free taste of another that they are likely to enjoy. As a result, Death Row's sales skyrocketed. Additionally, they have significantly shortened the time and investment required to launch a new artist.

When you go to the dentist, do you get a free toothbrush? I bet it's a specific brand that that dentist is getting for free to provide you with a positive impression of this brand. This leads to you possibly buying many from this brand in the future, based upon the lended-credibility and positive overall impression you get about this item.

How can you do this in your small business? Do you have free samples of collaborative products and services you can bundle with yours that make your solution more attractive?

Informational Marketing

Most marketing involves telling someone about your company, product or service with the hope that when they need this product or service they will think of your company. Informational marketing is completely different from what most marketers are doing today. It focuses on giving, not getting. It focuses on the needs of the *client.* Informational Marketing is effortless and works brilliantly for nearly any kind of product or service.

The benefits of informational marketing are both powerful and practical:

- Spend no time talking about what you do
- Learn what people need
- Attract the right kind of customers
- Become an authority and an influencer to your target audience
- Encourage people to do the right thing for themselves

Nearly any business can implement an informational marketing program. The first step is to send valuable, pertinent information to members of your target audience on a periodic basis. Many people hear this and immediately think of a newsletter, but while a newsletter may include pertinent information, it is rarely valuable or authoritative enough to create *influence*. But there is a formula that ensures your informational marketing message will both get attention and generate response, and perhaps most importantly, make you an *influencer* in your marketplace.

Informational Marketing Formula

Here is an example of the formula in action. This e-blast was sent to several thousand people who subscribed to our "Business Update," and we not only received record response, but it also attracted more listeners to the radio show on that date.

Opening
Have a compelling headline. Take a STAND! People like controversy

Death of a Family

1st Paragraph
Use an analogy. This makes it easier for readers to relate to your message and they want to learn more.

You've heard of the book, "Death of a Salesman." This article is about the death of a family. What does that have to do with running a small business, you ask? I'll get there in a moment. First, let me ask you a question. Is your business like a family?

Body
Use humor

I hear this all the time. "Mark, our business is different, it's just like a family." I know business owners and managers say this to communicate something positive about their company's culture. I think this is great! But I always smile when I hear this. I often want to ask, "Oh yeah, what kind of family is it like?" But I don't, because I'm practicing my Dale Carnegie principal of "letting the other person save face." I smile because the relationships within a company CAN be just as screwed-up as the relationships within a family.

Examples

Use examples to make your idea real.

> *For example, consider how favoritism can cripple the relationships within a family. It happens all the time. It's happening to families right now. The results are far-reaching and dramatic when one sibling is treated differently from another. The favored sibling feels that they are not as obligated to perform at a specific level in order to gain a specific reward. Since they are favored, they know from experience that they will not be held as accountable as the next sibling will. The rules can be bent for them. Everyone in the family knows this. Consequently, there is resentment, anger, hostility, and conflict. The unfavored sibling is no longer motivated to perform. No matter what they do, they cannot live up to the admiration the parent has for their brother or sister. This causes frustration and embarrassment. It can even result in vengeance and criminal activity in order to "get even." The "I'll show them" attitude.*
>
> *What makes favoritism so insidious is that it can be exercised in a very subtle manner. It may manifest itself in the WAY things are communicated. For example, imagine a circumstance where two siblings alternate weeks taking out the trash. When the unfavored sibling fails to take out the trash, the consequence may be for the parent to say, "I can't even depend on you to take out the trash." When the favored sibling fails to take out the trash, the consequence may be for the parent to say, "Just make sure you get it done next time." The favored sibling gets another chance, while the unfavored sibling's wholesale capabilities have been diminished. This is rarely done in a purposeful way or even through subterfuge. It happens on a subconscious*

> *level. Before we know it, the words are out and the damage is done.*

Correlation

Relate the examples directly to the reader's problem and resolution.

> *This works precisely the same way for a business organization. As owners and managers, our goal is to induce greater teamwork, a more harmonious workplace, and improved productivity. One of the most important factors in building teamwork is the leader's ability to implement what I call "equitable response." Equitable response is the leaders ability to react to every team member in the same manner in any specified circumstance. In other words, their ability to treat people relatively the same under any given set of circumstances. For example, don't allow one employee to arrive at work late because she lives further away or because she has to pick up the kids at school.*

Sound Bites

Use one-liners—"Sound Bites"—to drive your point home and make it easy to remember. Politicians and the media use "sound bites" to create interest and become more memorable. Why shouldn't you?

> *Credibility is lost when owners and managers are inconsistent in rewards and punishments.*

Application

Tell your audience how to apply the knowledge, and be *specific.* This places you in a position of authority—a position that *attracts* respect.

Here is what I counsel my clients to do:

1. Consistently reward positive behavior and punish negative behavior. CONSISTENTLY!

2. Don't allow yourself to be manipulated by employees.

3. Don't allow your personal opinions to influence the way you respond to team members. The fact that you may like or dislike them should NOT play a role in the reward/punishment process.

4. Let the time you spend with team members become part of the reward. Conversely you should limit the time spent with those team members that fail to maintain performance. Tell them what is expected in no uncertain terms. No idle chitchat.

5. Model competent behavior. They will do as you do, NOT as you say.

6. Provide consistent feedback and predictable consequences.

7. Set realistic and clear expectations.

Build Credibility

Now you've earned the right to talk about your solution and how it relates to the problem/resolution. But keep it brief.

In my consulting practice, I rarely see these things consistently being done in small companies. Often times owners and managers have a whole set of rules which apply to different people in the organization at different times. This causes confusion, stifles communication, hinders teamwork, and creates fear. It usually ends up

> *with excessive turnover and even anarchy. Sadly, the result is the death of a company family.*

Questions

Use the empathy process to end with questions bearing on a need.

> *Does this mean we shouldn't attempt to replicate the family atmosphere in our companies? Or should we replicate the model of the healthy family where everyone knows what is expected of him or her and everyone is rewarded and punished with equanimity?*
>
> *How healthy is your company family?*
>
> *What are you doing to foster a healthy family business environment?*

Credits

Demonstrate that you have taken the time to research this issue and give credit where the credit is due.

> *My best to you this week,*
> *Mark Deo*
>
> **** This article was inspired by my mentor and colleague, Morrie Shechtman, author of the bestseller, "Working Without a Net" and former advisor to the Speaker of the House.*
>
> **** Hear Morrie speak with me about "Relationship Building in a High Risk Culture" on July 15, 2006 at 7am on 97.1FM*

Free Offer

Try to offer something for free to give people an incentive to come closer into your "inner circle of influence."

> ***FREE SMALL-BIZ SUCCESS MANUAL***
>
> *Now offering the first installment of our Small Business Success Manual. The cost is $0! That's right, it's FREE. After just two to three weeks of implementing the techniques in this manual you will already be attracting more business. (Which is a lot better than cold calling!) This will give you just a taste of what we do to help fellow entrepreneurs.*

Pitch

Now give your promotional messages in an informational way rather than a feature/benefit salesy approach.

> ***Listen to Mark on the Small Business Hour on 97.1FM every Sunday at 7am***
>
> *Can't listen to the show on Sundays at 7AM? NO PROBLEM - - - Now you can catch Mark 24 hours per day! - - - Listen to the Small Business Hour online with just the click of a button any time you want. We post Sundays show every Monday morning.*
>
> *Fresh from Oprah and Sally Jessie Raphael appearances, Rhonda Britten, the country's leading authority on personal empowerment, talks to Mark on Sunday at 7am on 97.1FM. Call in and win a FREE autographed, hardbound copy of "Fearless Living."*
>
> **** Check out our great new line up of guests. - - - Just go to: Schedule on our home page or click on http://www.sbanetwork.org/radio*

Contact Information

Tell them how to reach you and include your branding statement

Copyright 2006, Mark Deo. All rights reserved.

Mark Deo
Host - CBS Radio's Small Business Hour - Sundays, 7 AM, KLSX, 97.1FM

Answers for your small business at: http://www.smallbusinesshour.com/

Helping companies make better decisions: http://www.markdeo.com

Even this book contains a "FREE Bonus." If you turn to the back of the book you will see that the next step in engaging YOU as a loyal member of the Rules of Attraction system is to entice you to learn more about how these Rules can be used in your business life to add greater value. This "FREE Bonus" includes case studies, an online video, our Business Assessment tool, our Podcast and more. We encourage you to claim these bonuses at www.markdeo.com/rulesofattraction.

You can also include a "FREE Bonus" with your product or service. This can build loyalty and reward your most frequent customers and visitors.

Personal Action Plan

- What is it that you can "give away" that will create attraction?
- How can you bring an elephant to city hall in order to get noticed in a positive way?
- Identify a partner that you can work with in bundling a related solution with your own which will make you BOTH more attractive?

- Develop your own informational marketing program that uses the formula discussed above.
- Create your first informational e-blast and test it with your subscribers.
- Think of some "FREE Bonuses" that you can offer to loyal customers.

Rule #7:

Reverse Risk

Viral Envy

"I hate to say it, but he's got more buzz than we do," declared Mrs. Hilary Clinton.

It's fitting that a Presidential candidate whose platform was focused so clearly on "change," would be the first to use viral methods so effectively in his primary campaign. Not only was Barack Obama a breakthrough candidate in this regard, he used these methods to accomplish Rule #6: to reduce the voters' risk in changing. His viral marketing community has grown to include LinkedIn, MySpace, Facebook, and his army of bloggers and commentators has effectively blanketed online venues with a presence of supporters. No campaign has been more aggressive in tapping into social networks and leveraging the financial power of hundreds of thousands of small donors. President Barack Obama racked-up more than $40 million in campaign contributions from over 300,000 constituents. More than $10 million of these were made online, and ninety percent of them were in increments of $100 or less. This demonstrates that he reached more potential voters on-line than any other candidate in history.

Obama reversed the risk of the Democratic voter in a powerful way. With everything against him—he's a Black American, with a Muslim background, lacking substantial wealth compared to other candidates, and lacking in significant political experience—his campaign was so viral that even his contenders were amazed. He even personally posted numerous questions to his constituents on the various social networks such as LinkedIn using them as a channel for political outreach. This strategy was more powerful than making statements about his policies or political positions on issues because it opened a space wherein voters could (theoretically) interact with him. This sense of connection and interaction reverses the sense of risk that accompanies selecting a relative newcomer on the political scene as the Democratic candidate for the Presidency. Moves like this one cause Obama to be seen as a "man of the people," and, for young people especially, placing himself in such a venue demonstrates his awareness of new technology. The belief that Obama was hip is due to such viral presences. His face, name, and brand were spread across the nation—and it happened without spending a dime. Could it be that using the Rules of Attraction made him President?

Making Application

The term "risk-reversal" typically has application in the financial community, as the manner in which foreign exchange options are quoted by finance dealers. Instead of quoting these options' prices, dealers quote their volatility. The greater the demand for an options contract, the greater its volatility and its price. A positive risk reversal means the volatility of calls is greater than the volatility of similar puts. But you can easily see how the concept moves across disciplines. In Obama's case, he has hedged his entire campaign on the fact that young voters believe that the older options (Clinton, McCain, Giuliani, Edwards) are all cut from the same cloth and as such, they were more volatile than he was.

What is true in marketing a political contender to voters can also be true in marketing your product or service to prospects. Often the reasons prospects are hesitant to change suppliers or service providers is the inherent risk involved in that change. Their concern is twofold: if they make a change in favor of your solution, valuable time will be spent, while their situation may not improve; and, worse, they may spend the valuable time and see their situation become worse. The goal is to reverse the risk they feel and make it excitement and *attraction.* They must feel comfortable making a change, and thus we must create a way for them to feel that any risk is eliminated. There are several ways that we can do this:

- Leveraging Volatility
- Free Trials
- Guarantees

Leveraging Volatility

If we can help prospects to view competitors as offering more volatile solution then we can potentially reverse their risk in changing. This is precisely what Obama did in his bid for the presidency. Yet this can be applied to any discipline.

For example, imagine you are an aerospace manufacturer attempting to win a government contract for a particular component. This component is currently under manufacture by one of your competitors. You have information about their lack of reliability in terms of delivery. So you focus a greater part of your marketing efforts on how you will ensure delivery, the reliability of the type of delivery system you will employ, and even incentives that reward the customer if you are in fact unable to perform to the expected delivery timeline. This obviously will increase the likelihood of your winning this contract. You are leveraging the volatility of delivery against your competitors' ability to perform.

Leveraging volatility is very different than torpedoing the reputation of your competitor, which is always unacceptable, and will often backfire anyway. Besides violating Rule #11 (Stay tuned!), your customer will likely lose confidence in *your* character. Instead, we must approach creating volatility with a positive mindset.

Successfully leveraging volatility requires that we use two other rules of attraction very effectively: Rule number two (make the problem more important than the solution) and Rule number one (become a bigger fish in a small pond).

Without a firm understanding of the problem, we will not be able to create volatility in the mind of the buyer. We must ensure that the buyer sees their current circumstance as an obstacle in achieving their ultimate goals. Though it seems obvious, this emphasis is often overlooked by well-meaning marketers who will often concentrate exclusively on their solution, thus failing to have the customer agree with them, and failing to remind the customer of the pain that the problem initiates.

In addition, we must have a good understanding of the competitive landscape in order to effectively leverage volatility. If we *think* that our competitor is volatile and in fact they are not, then all of our investments and efforts in creating a sense of volatility will be in vain. If the competitor in fact performs sufficiently in solving the customer's problems, then our solution seems redundant in the eyes of the customer. This is why understanding and completing the competitive landscape profile in the earlier chapter of this book is absolutely critical before you attempt to create a risk reversal strategy.

Creating volatility is just as applicable for a small company as it is for the large aerospace manufacturer discussed above. Let's assume for a moment, you are a remodeling contractor. Your competition is similar to you in every way except they typically leave a mess at the job site. You hate messes and therefore are rather particular about how the job site is left at the end of the day. Since your customers are homeowners who must live in their home while the construction project is in process, a messy job site can cause a great deal of hardship and dissatisfaction. So you attempt to create volatility by demonstrating how clean you leave the job site. In fact, you are so confident that your crew will leave the jobsite spotless that you are willing to pay each customer $100 for every scrap of garbage left at the site. You offer: if they find a tool out of place you will allow them to keep it. This is a compelling way to leverage volatility for those interested in a clean environment. And not once did you slip in an underhanded insult toward the competition.

In short, creating volatility is a powerful way to reverse the customer's risk in changing. Let's look at a few other ways to accomplish the same result.

Free Trials

This risk reversal method is often used in the software business. A while back I was taking a look at a software program to use in conjunction with managing my coaches and consultants in the field. I found what I thought to be a great software program which would allow me to track their schedule, results of their meetings, billable hours, follow-up item and then upload the information to my accounting software automatically. I read through the information pages and sales page.

Then I hesitated half an inch from the shopping cart. Why? Price. At $600, the program is not inexpensive. The company had done all they could to sell me the software. Now they just had to reverse the risk and remove my anxiety about paying that much. They accomplished this with an offer of a 30-day free trial. They further increase their chances of having me purchase by not requesting my address, or my credit card number. No small print said quietly, "You will be billed at the end of 30 days if you don't cancel." They simply enabled me to try the software free for 30 days—no strings attached.

Using this type of risk reversal is intended to remove the perfectly natural anxiety that has become our instinct before purchasing—particularly if one is purchasing from a new vendor. However, it is not a magic bullet that covers the sin of sales copy with anxiety-increasing messages. We must be careful—in some cases, the risk reversal device *itself* can cause anxiety. For example, the software manufacturer could have asked for all kinds of personal information, including my credit card number, and then billed my credit card if I didn't cancel before 30 days. In that case, the offer itself would have created anxiety and I would not have purchased. Simply because, like many others, I know my tendency to forget.

Experiment with this type of risk reversal—but be brave with it. Risk is reversed only if all our messages are consistently making the customer feel safe.

Guarantees

Guarantees are probably the oldest and most misused form of risk reversal. The more compelling the guarantee, the less risk your customer will perceive. It is important to understand that while you may be offering a strong guarantee, it doesn't mean that all of your customers will take you up on it. In fact, studies have shown that less that two percent of all clients cash in on the very guarantee that motivated their buying decision. You probably already have a strong guarantee that you've forgotten to promote.

Sample Guarantee

Remember Pelican Products, the manufacturers of indestructible cases and flashlights. Their slogan, if you recall, is: "*You break it. We replace it. Forever.*" This guarantee is unmatched in their industry and their competitors are stymied by their inability to match it. $100 million in business this year for Pelican (read: it helps to have a powerful guarantee!)

Results Oriented Guarantee

Providing a guarantee of specific results is the most powerful type of guarantee. This might include a guarantee of timely performance, error free operation, asset appreciation, or financial value. The more specific the guaranteed benefits or results, the less risk will be perceived. This requires citing some evidence so that prospects can understand precisely how the guarantee ensures the results. Here are a few examples:

A very common guarantee is: "*Either you're completely satisfied or we'll give you your money back*". The reason this type of guarantee is so popular is that very few people take advantage of it. It's more inconvenient and time consuming for people to request their money back than it is for them to suck it up and move on. Often people will be hesitant to admit to themselves that they are dissatisfied with the purchase. Their egos get in the way. If they request their money back, they are admitting to themselves and others that they made a mistake in making the purchase, and that they need the money enough to ask for it back. This kind of guarantee is often constructed using very powerful language such as:

"I'm so convinced that you'll be absolutely delighted with your purchase, that I'm prepared to give you an ironclad 120 day, totally outrageous, take it or leave it guarantee."

This type of compelling language and commitment often is enough to reverse the inherent risk for the buyer.

Non-Results Oriented Guarantee

Examples of these type of guarantees are "hassle free," "personal guarantee," "guaranteed customer satisfaction," and "conditional guarantees" (if you do this, we'll do that). These types of guarantees are not as strong as "results-based" guarantees, as we discussed above, because some portion of the burden remains upon the buyer: a risk residue.

Giveaways

Giveaways are very effective ways to reduce risk and to overcome procrastination. By giving away part of our solution, we build credibility with the buyer and allow them to try out our solution. This leverages two powerful forces in the marketing process. The first is utilizing the word *FREE*. While it may be overused, the word "free" still carries a powerful effect over those that hear it. The second is when we give something to someone, they automatically feel obligated to give something back. It's only human nature.

I have seen countless examples of this in action:

- The auto repair center that gives away free oil changes. Valued at $69 each, these giveaways generate a good many new customers that purchase several thousand dollars in services each year.

- Consultants or professionals that offer a free introductory assessment.
- Software companies that offer free trialware or "shareware".

Combination Strategies

While guarantees help to reverse risk and giveaways overcome procrastination, imagine how powerful both techniques can be when combined.

Here is a great example of a guarantee and a giveaway in the same offer for a search engine marketing company:

> *"Join our search engine optimization newsletter and you're automatically entered in a drawing for a Gold Search Engine Optimization Package valued at over $2,999. We're giving away one Gold search engine marketing package every month! We guarantee first page ranking on several major search engines. Click here to request a first page ranking proposal."*

Regardless of the type of guarantee you offer, every product or service should incorporate a risk reversal strategy into their marketing campaign. We spend considerably more time on this in our Attract More Business program, Tele-clinics and in our one-on-one Tele-coaching, because it is at the core of successful sales.

Just ask the President of the United States.

Personal Action Plan:

- What risk do your prospects take in selecting you as an option?
- How can you use volatility as a risk reversal strategy?
- What can you offer as a free trial to motivate prospects to try your solution? How can you lock-them-in?

- What type of guarantees can you offer that would be appealing to your customers and prospects?
- What is your plan to incorporate risk reversals into your marketing strategy?

Rule #8:

Let Design and Color Speak

Take a Drink

"So what's different about your water?" I asked.

He slapped the bottle of clear liquid on the conference room table and said, "Just look at it!"

My client, Bill Flegenheimer, and I sat staring at the bottle, trying hard to figure out what was different.

"Oh yeah," I said. "It's square."

The man smiled. And Fiji water was born in the United States.

Bill has been my client for nearly twenty years and over the course of that period he has employed all fourteen Rules of Attraction. He is a Customers Broker and has built a nice business particularly by using Rule # 1 more effectively than perhaps anyone I've known. He has "become a bigger fish in a smaller pond" by narrowing his market to only perishable products. So instead of pursuing importers of hard-goods, technology and textiles, he strictly focuses on perishable products like meat, seafood, produce and, of course, water. His expertise caught the interest of the folks at Fiji, which is how we were all sitting in a conference room staring at a square bottle of water.

Bottled water is a phenomenon of our times. When I was young (during the pre-digital Age) we would drink tap water and think nothing of it. How is it possible that millions of us will pay good money—often two or three dollars a bottle—for a product we have always gotten, and can still get, for *free*?

Studies have proven it: bottled water isn't healthier, or safer, than tap water. According to *Fast Company* (I told you: the coolest magazine on the planet!), while the United States is the single biggest consumer in the world's $50 billion bottled-water market, it is the only *one* of the top *four*—the others are Brazil, China, and Mexico—that has universally reliable tap water. Tap water in this country, with rare exceptions, is impressively safe. It is monitored constantly, and the test results made public. According to NationMaster.com, an on-line data source, the average American drinks 18 half-liter bottles of water per month, far more than coffee, milk or beer. This makes the entire bottled-water industry about half the size of the carbonated beverage industry.

When we buy a bottle of water, what we're buying is the bottle itself as much as the water inside. We are buying the *creative story* that the water companies are telling us. For example, in Fiji, where Fiji water is bottled, there is a state-of-the-art factory which churns out more than *a million bottles a day,* primarily for the U.S. market. Yet more than half the people in Fiji do not have safe, reliable drinking water. A sad fact, and a hidden one, because American consumers are willing to spend billions not based on reality, but on a dream, not on the product, but on the story. The square bottle supported the story; it is the design of the Fiji bottle that singles them out from the hundreds of other bottled drinking water available.

Giant Brand, Guerilla Tactics

Perhaps you recognize the illustration style? It won critical acclaim from the design world for the Oscar winner *Walk the Line* in 2005.

Designed by artist Shepard Fairey, it never would have happened were it not for the wrestler Andre the Giant.

Thanks to my associate and younger counterpart at SBA Network, Matt Walker, I am forced to engage with art, music, and trends that impact younger people. I kept noticing a particular style of artwork that caught my attention, and asked Matt, the pop-culture guru. And I heard the name Shepard Fairey for the first time. If you're under 35, you've likely seen Fairey's art, and might even be quite familiar with it; if over, you've still probably seen it, but you may have ignored it. Shepard Fairey's remarkable branding campaign began in Rhode Island in 1989 as a joke. A student at the Rhode Island School of Design, Fairey created a silhouette of the famed wrestler Andre the Giant to show a friend how silhouettes could be made of virtually any photo. As a joke, he decided to place the image on a sticker, with the text *7'4", 520 LB., Andre the Giant has a Posse*. Intended to mock underground skateboarding culture, these stickers were placed all over Providence, Rhode Island—on the back of street signs, streetlights, traffic signals, buildings, etc.

Receiving a great deal of feedback from friends in the skating community, Shepard took out an ad in a skateboarding magazine featuring the image and a P.O. Box, with a note urging people to send a Self Addressed Stamped Envelope for more information. He would send back a few stickers, a template to use for printing more, and a note urging the recipient to spread the message.

I can recall personally seeing these stickers in Pittsburgh, PA in 1992, as well as in Los Angeles in the early '90s. Shepard Fairey then transitioned into a more stylized image, and created other silhouette styled images that were incorporated into posters that mock government propaganda with the word "Obey" featured prominently.

Since then, his work has been seen in numerous films (including *Batman Forever*, *8 MM*, and others), and he is now designing CD covers, movie posters, t-shirts, and has built a visual brand among persons who were young adults from the late 80s until now.

Shepard Fairey created a brand *without* a product, only a style of design. When he started, he had nothing to sell. He's created a legion of fans who spread his message for him. Whether you like or dislike his tactics (many view it as simple vandalism), the result cannot be denied: mainstream commercial success. Fairey was even asked by President Obama's campaign marketers to develop a gritty poster that could be used to make the candidate more attractive to the younger crowd who were more familiar with Fairey's artistic style. To make the power of the image even more captivating, the single four letter word – HOPE was added. This drove home the meaning of the image and aligned Obama with what the younger people in America wanted in a candidate, "hope for the future."

Design First

Image is a tremendous way to tap into your intuitive mind for a simple solution to your problem. For years, most marketers have dealt with advertising and promotional challenges by first creating a "copy concept" then giving it to a designer to "make it pretty." That is, the design elements were added last, as an afterthought, an obligatory addendum. But today design is leading the marketing process. Design the ad first—regardless of what your developing. A fast, dirty, unfiltered design sketch will create a model that will help you think through the solution to the problem on several levels.

Management guru Tom Peters is bullish on design. He is also a proponent of design-first in the marketing realm. His book, *Re-Imagine* not only spends considerable time talking about how and why design is so critical to marketing success, it also offers all 250 pages of the book in full color, with beautiful photos and illustrations.

We know that a picture tells a story, but we don't trust it. So we use words to tell the story, and an image to augment that story. I'd like to suggest that this model be inverted; let the art of design tell the story, and use words only to augment that story.

As digital production and publishing becomes more and more affordable, we will see design oriented books and publications become more prolific. Even this book is a testament to the digital publishing revolution. In the past, publishers would print hundreds of thousands of books using the traditional lithographic or off-set print technology. It was impossible to print a few books on a litho press without incurring massive cost. This is because the technology depends upon economies of scale to make it affordable. If you've ever seen an offset printing press run, you know precisely what I mean. Today, publishers are employing what is known in the industry as POD, or "print on demand." Since there are no longer huge economies of scale in digital printing, publishers can print books as needed, immediately. That means when a book is ordered by a bookstore or on-line, the book is printed and sent to the customer within a matter of days. This reduces inventory, eliminates waste and ensures that the product is always available.

Design Tells the Story

For some companies, design and design only sets them apart. *Volkswagen*'s Bug, the Hummer, Scion (or the Good Humor truck as I like to call it), and Chrysler's entire line of retro vehicles.

Bang and Olfson created a line of consumer electronics products that offered nothing but a cool design. And they managed to sell their product for forty to fifty percent higher than the market price. In an industry driven by price erosion, they eliminated any price competition. When I worked for my father's company, Marantz they set their audio product apart by creating design elements that were exclusive like, gold anodized faceplates, rubber coated gyro touch tuning and walnut or maple side panels. The performance of the audio equipment was accentuated and communicated through the design of the product itself. This can be applied to nearly any product and even to services.

Color Branding

Imagine that you are at the airport waiting for a car rental or hotel shuttle. From a good distance, you can immediately determine which shuttle is yours. Marriott is red, Budget is blue, Alamo is yellow. Even the signs for each shuttle are color-branded for ease of recognition. Checker Taxi built their entire brand identity—as well as their name—on their yellow checkered cabs. Remember Apple's rainbow logo? It was a perfect reflection of the brand: reflecting creativity, differentiation, diversity, and fun. Some companies use a color in their names: jetBlue, Red Cross, Pink, Yellow Pages and so on. This helps to reinforce the identity and create top-of-the-mind awareness: when people *see* the color, they *think* the brand.

While IBM is associated with the most common corporate color, blue, UPS has chosen one of the least-used colors, brown, and turned it into a tremendous brand asset. Its Valentine's Delivery press release was titled "Roses are Brown." Many color experts agree that "brown" represents steadfastness, simplicity, friendliness and dependability. These attributes are perfect for a company like UPS. In addition "brown" is quite a unique color in branding, as very few companies use brown as their corporate color. Thus, UPS has come to use it as a moniker, "brown" is an appellation! In its latest series of ads, it replaced the corporate name with "brown" in the tag line: "What can brown do for you?" That's color branding at its best.

Some companies literally *own* their own colors. Tiffany and Company has registered its trademark robin's egg blue as a brand asset. This box has come to represent the highest quality in jewelry and the box alone demands a higher price. Burberry's plaid is trademarked as well, and so recognizable the world over that men and women in New York leave their trenches unbuttoned so that when the wind blows, the plaid lining is visible.

Color cannot be underestimated as a brand asset, helping clients and prospects recognize you. But color can be used to support goals far beyond simply recognition. It can be used to evoke emotion and build that all-important connection with the people who surround your brand. You can use color to further differentiate your organization from your competitors, revitalize an aging product and engage and unite your employees, partners and customers. When you go beyond the traditional use of color, you can make incredible strides in achieving your goals.

Selecting Your Colors

A color can be connected to a product, like Tide's bold orange box evokes vibrancy. Consider the meaning of the following colors in your business marketing:

- White: Pure. Clean. Youthful. A neutral color that can imply purity in fashion and sterilization in the medical profession.
- Black: Power. Elegant. Secretive. Can target your high-end market or be used in youth marketing to add mystery to your image.
- Red: Passion. Excitement. Danger. The color of attention, causing the blood pressure and heart rate to rise. Use red to inject excitement into your brand.
- Orange: Vibrant. Energy. Play. Add some fun to your company if you want to create a playful environment for your customers.
- Yellow: Happy. Warm. Alert. Yellow can be an attractor for your business with a relaxed feeling.
- Green: Natural. Healthy. Plentiful. To create a calming effect or growth image choose green. Go green.
- Purple: Royalty. Wise. Celebration. Maybe add some purple tones to your look for your premium service business.
- Blue: Loyal. Peaceful. Trustworthy. Blue is the most popular and neutral color on a global scale. A safe choice for a business building customer loyalty.

While these basic color principles are critical when it comes to corporate design, many business leaders tend to over simplify the importance and sophistication of proper use of color and design, believing it to be a personal or subjective component. In reality, there is a right and wrong way to use color in corporate design. This is where the help of a professional designer can be quite valuable.

The Problem with Marketing Design

Publishers and librarians are engaged in near daily lamentation: we live in a post-literate world. Few read newspapers; fewer still read books. We definitely don't have time to read marketing material, be it an ad, Web site, e-blast or brochure. We need to get the concept at first *glance*. Most people are visually oriented (remember the left brain, right brain discussion?), and if we can use color and design properly, we can get the attention of more people, become more memorable, and create a powerful impression that makes people *feel*, and motivates them to take action.

Even with the appropriate color selection in your branding and marketing material, most businesses, large and small, fail to use design to create *attraction* in their marketing efforts. In fact, as I've said earlier, most marketing materials, *even professionally prepared material*, are very poorly prepared. The message is rarely clear, concise, compelling, credible, relevant, or unique. In addition, it fails in four other key areas:

1. Wrong Orientation – focused on *what we do* rather than *what they get*
2. Weak Content – not enough information to persuade, contains poor or no evidence
3. Tasteless Layout or Design – creates the wrong image and difficult to read
4. Typos and Grammatical Errors – damages credibility

Here's how to recognize and rectify these shortcomings.

How Materials should be used:

1. Mailed to prospects after they have called you
2. Mailed to associates with a cover letter to inform them of your services
3. Available on the web for those that are referred to you
4. Available to prospects that find you though search engines, AdWords, or Internet advertising
5. Seen or heard in a radio, TV or print advertisement

Whether you are creating a brochure, video, DVD or CD, print ad, radio or TV advertising, or simply a flyer, mailer, or fax, it is important that we create an ad design first. Even though our goal may be to create a simple brochure that explains our product or service, if we create an ad design first, we can ensure that our brochure will get attention and focus on addressing the client's problems and solving them in a believable way.

Headlines

Position is established in marketing by the wise use of headlines. Most marketing or advertising communications have a headline. The headline is typically designed to "get attention." In some cases, a compelling visual is used to get attention and the headline draws the reader into the copy text. The following are some approaches that we can take in the development of the headline:

- **Problem** – Focuses on the problem that the prospect is facing, thereby increasing acknowledgment of their pain.
- **Solution** – Focuses on the solutions or benefits that the company, product or service provides; the salve for the pain
- **Motive** – Focuses on not so much "what" the customer wants but "why" they want it.

- **Analogies** – A clever or creative way of explaining the problem, solution, or motive which the marketing device is attempting to communicate.
- **Combination** – These headlines use a combination of strategies such as a problem/solution ad or an analogy that explains the problem or a motive that uses an analogy.

After selecting one of the approaches to creating the headline it is important that we follow some of the basic rules of headline creation:

Do be:

- Targeted – Speak directly to your target audience.
- Compelling – Make your argument persuasive by supporting it with evidence.
- Concise – Don't ramble. Get to the point.

Don't Use:

- Clichés – Cute and clever statements are often redundant and have become worn out. They may bring a smile but, more likely, they won't be noticed at all, and will ring as empty, thus failing to communicate the message or be memorable.
- Qualitative statement – Statements like: biggest, best, award-winning, state-of-the-art, exceptional, unsurpassed, high quality, top-performing and so on are not believable. Additionally, these types of statements are so over-used that they might as well be invisible. They are all claims and are far less effective than facts. Remember that whatever you say you need to be prepared to back-up with incontrovertible evidence.
- Double-entendres often roll off the tongue nicely but can be a roller coaster ride for the mouth. If you use a double-entendre, you had better make it creative, highly relevant, and very memorable.

After writing the headline it is necessary to create a sub-headline. The sub-headline should serve to clarify the headline and affect the visual transition from the headline to the copy. The sub-headline must make it easier for the reader to understand the purpose of the ad or marketing device.

Even if you have no experience in developing ads or marketing material, you can follow a very simple formula for creating this type of material. Ads and marketing communication material (or MARCOM) typically must contain five elements:

- Status – This communicates the current condition.
- Implication – This implies how things may get worse and how the pain might increase if things continue.
- Appeal – This presents the solution in a way that appeals to the logical or emotional motive or desire for change.
- Evidence – Proof that the solution that you are offering does work. This proof comes in the form of a testimonial, analogy, statistics, an example of a client success, demonstration, or an exhibit.
- Call to Action – What action do you want people to take after hearing or seeing your ad?

Design Layout 101

Even if you have no design experience, your gut will lead you true. Have you ever noticed that some ads are very pleasing to the eye, while others look like a bundle of words and images spread all over the page? That's your gut, and it can often be trusted, if it's guided a bit. The following is a good trainer.

- Primary image – This photograph or illustration should dominate the ad, consuming anywhere from 1/3 to 2/3 of the ad. The primary image, along with the headline, is responsible for gaining attention.
- Secondary image – The secondary image should be no larger than twenty percent of the size of the primary image. Otherwise, it might compete with the primary image, weakening both.

- Headline – The headline should complement the image by clarifying it, establishing our position, and drawing the reader into the copy.
- Sub-headline – It is not always necessary to use a sub-headline; however, they can clarify the headline and make it easier for the reader to understand how the headline and the image relate to their challenge.
- Body copy – This powerfully and succinctly communicates our message in the fewest words possible. Use active tense, simple words, and avoid clichés. Make sure that you use language designed for your target audience.
- Call to action – This tells the reader/listener/viewer what action they should take and gives them an incentive for doing so.
- Logo assembly –This should be consistent in all forms of communication. It should contain the logo, meme or tag line, and the name of the company. It is important that this be done in the same way at all times and in all forms of execution.

In addition to the above formula there are several strategies to marketing visual development that you can take. Below, I'll give you a look at some specific examples that demonstrate precisely how some products and services have used these strategies:

1. Shocking – Uses striking visuals and/or perhaps a shocking or controversial image.
2. Collage – Group of images centered on a theme or a story. It is difficult, however, to create a visual center and smooth read with several images. Expert help suggested!
3. Personal – Photos of people in order to increase their visibility and make them more recognizable. Sometimes brands are centered around a specific person.

4. Endearing – Photos of children, pets, babies, and couples in love can be very compelling when accompanied with the right headline.
5. Illustration – I only recommend using illustrations if you have a professional designer on the job. Amateur illustrations simply lessen credibility.
6. Royalty Free Photos – Over-used or stock photos also reduce credibility and adversely affect ad effectiveness.

Recognizing What Works

Conceptual conversation is important, but nothing's more effective than concrete critique. So let's take a look at some specific marketing campaigns and examine what works and what doesn't. The purpose: to put together advertising and marketing communications that blow away your competition by using the tools you've been given.

Before and After

Take a look at some of the advertisements shown on the following pages. I obtained permission to reprint these ads from two very prominent yellow page advertising companies – Max Effect (www.max-effect.com) and AdRevamp (www.adrevamp.com). These organizations are in the business of re-designing ads that *don't work* into ads that *DO work*. They provide a compelling example of advertisements that are effective as compared to those which are not. The color version of these ads can also be seen at www.markdeo.com/rulesofattraction.

Day Care Center - Before Ad
- re-printed with permission of Max Effect -www.max-effect.com.

The first ad (Day Care Center – Before Ad) adheres to none of the rules we've discussed. It was developed without any consideration to the aforementioned strategies. The focus of the ad is "Established in 1970." Who cares? It says "day care center" but I already know that this is a day care center since that is the section of the phone book in which the ad appears. It is jammed with copy and bullet points which impedes understanding of the central components of the message. Finally the ad includes a laundry list of features such as State Licensed, New Facility, Trained Staff and so on. However these are not benefit oriented in any way.

Day Care Center - After Ad
- re-printed with permission of Max Effect (www.max-effect.com).

The next ad (Day Care Center – After Ad), on the contrary clearly focuses on the solution to the problem: "Will I be comfortable with my baby there?" It is targeted, compelling, obvious, concise and uses a striking visual. The image of the baby's face is simple, appealing and endearing to the reader. This is a great example of how a "single" quality image can be more compelling than a series of clip-art images. What is most powerful about this re-design is that it boosted response and it didn't cost one more penny to run. I encourage you to go to www.markdeo.com/rulesofattraction to see the "After" ad in color and compare it to the "Before" ad.

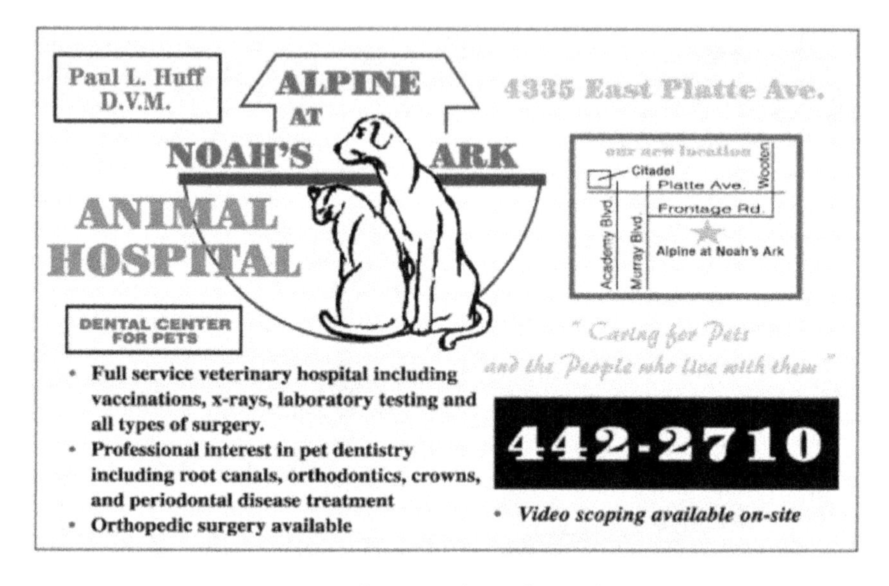

Animal Hospital - Before Ad
- re-printed with permission of Max Effect (www.max-effect.com).

Is that supposed to be an ark with animals on it? This is an example of how home-made artwork can destroy your message. Not only is the art and layout tasteless but the entire ad is filled with copy. There is no negative space to guide the reader's eye to the critical message. As with most of the "Before" ads that we will see, it does not focus on what the reader "gets" but rather on what the advertiser "does." This is a critical error. We have reproduced this "before" ad in black and white, yet the color version can be viewed on our web site at www.markdeo.com/rulesofattraction.

Animal Hospital - After Ad
- re-printed with permission of Max Effect (www.max-effect.com).

The after ad is far better. It is very attractive with cute animals and it hits the motive of taking care of your pet on the nose (no pun intended). While it cannot be seen in this black and white version, the designers put the phone number in red which makes it more apparent, especially for the yellow pages. In the Before version it is quickly apparent that this ad incorporates more than four colors. The ad cost a fortune because the color is used very poorly. It does not use the four-color blending process of CMYK (cyan, magenta, yellow and Black) but rather uses the special PMS colors for specific text and images. This actually impedes the visual appeal of the ad and significantly increases the cost. The After ad incorporates four color process which makes it more appealing to the eye.

Auto Dealership - Before Ad
- re-printed with permission of AdRevamp (www.adrevamp.com).

This ad defines itself as tawdry with the headline, "Used Autos." It almost looks like they just threw their ideas on paper and called it a day. There are over five fonts which creates a very confused look. In addition the most important and emotional part of the ad is the postage size photo of the automobile.

Auto Dealership - After Ad
- re-printed with permission of AdRevamp (www.adrevamp.com).

The After ad on the other hand uses the Problem/Solution format that we discussed earlier. While the ad does focus on price it pulls the reader in with a compelling image of the vehicle dominating the ad and the headline and copy wrapping nicely. The Better Business Bureau logo adds credibility and it uses only three fonts which gives it a clean, organized feel.

Heating and AC - Before Ad
- re-printed with permission of AdRevamp (www.adrevamp.com).

This ad for a heating and air conditioning service utilizes very feature-oriented rather than benefit-oriented copy which commoditizes the service. The headline uses a drop shadow which is far too large and impedes readership. The photo of the Maytag repairman is depressing and worrisome. He looks like no matter how he's tried he just can't fix the air conditioner. The Maytag logo looks like it was added at the last minute and the fonts are hard to read and confusing.

Heating and AC - After Ad
- re-printed with permission of AdRevamp (www.adrevamp.com).

The After ad is much more appealing and communicates the message in a powerful way with visuals alone. The Maytag logo is executed in a credible way and the copy is oriented toward the client benefits of the ten year and five year warranties. Finally this ad has a powerful call to action as we discussed earlier.

SPEED SHIP

PACKAGING • GIFTWRAP

POSTAL SERVICES

• CRATING
• PICK-UP SERVICE IN 94901
• FAX / COPIES
• UPS / FED EX / AND MORE !
• MAIL BOXES
• INSURED SHIPPING
• PACKING MATERIALS

415 721-7020

898 LINCOLN AVE • SAN RAFAEL

OPEN MONDAY - FRIDAY 8 AM - 6 PM
SATURDAY 9 AM - 5 PM

Postal Center - Before Ad
- re-printed with permission of AdRevamp (www.adrevamp.com).

The Before ad for "Speed Ship" makes an attempt to be uniform, organized and motivating yet it falls short of communicating why I should choose them over another shipping service. In addition all of the type is in capital letters. Again, this impedes readership greatly as compared to initial –capitalized type. This font style is very old and makes the ad look stale. The use of the muddy and tiny clip art fails to create any attention or differentiation.

Postal Center - After Ad
- re-printed with permission of AdRevamp (www.adrevamp.com).

The re-worked ad incorporates sharp visuals that tells the reader that they can ship by Fedex or UPS. The headline reinforces the fact that customers can do this "Fast and Easy." The credit cards and bold phone number create a powerful call to action.

Background Check - After Ad -
re-printed with permission of SBA Network, Inc. www.sbanetwork.com

This is an ad our agency prepared for a client that was devastatingly successful. It uses the "problem/solution" combination style previously mentioned. The image speaks volumes and the headline merely pushes readers to the copy. This ad is also shown to demonstrate that modifying images using Photoshop is an art. Don't try this at home. Leave the art to the artists. This ad works because the photo manipulation is tasteful and realistic. The ad also has a powerful exclusive marketing position statement. At the time, no one was offering a three to five day turnaround on a background check.

Advertising Exercise

Let's look at the cosmetic surgery industry again just for the sake of consistency. We will use our above formula to evaluate the headlines, sub-headline, copy, visuals, and layout of the following ads. Using what you know about the Rules, can you identify the strengths and weaknesses of the following ad?

Here is my initial evaluation of this ad:

Headline: States the obvious. Doesn't focus on the problem, solution or the motive.

Sub-Headline: Does not clarify the headline. How does innovation of art and science help me?

Copy: There is no emotional appeal, It's all about the advertiser not the reader. No evidence.

Visuals: Scary!! This is a perfect example of how a poorly done illustration can remove all credibility. If I'm spending thousands of dollars on a surgical procedure, the last thing I want is my face re-arranged like a puzzle!

Design/Layout: No logo assembly, No branding. Who is providing this service?

How would you change the ad? Answer the following questions:

1. What would you change so that it has the correct orientation?
2. What compelling images would you include?
3. How would you create problem/solution, motive, or analogy oriented headlines?
4. What would you include as appropriate body copy?
5. How would you properly layout this ad?

Personal Action Plan

Complete the section below and log on to www.markdeo.com/rulesofattraction to upload your ad and see some of the other re-designed ads.

Headline:

Sub-Headline:

Copy:

Visuals:

Design/Layout:

Rule #9:

Win Heartshare

My Friend Says I'm Crazy

"You're insane, Mark," my old schoolmate (and now multi-millionaire) told me. "I'm a successful businessman and you can't convince me that intangible assets are more valuable than tangible ones. I'll take real estate, equipment, inventory and cash over ideas, experiences and influence any day! You've been living in California too long."

Now when Mike spoke, most people in New Jersey listened. He owned and operated the Budweiser distributorship for the state. To those unaware of the power of an exclusive alcohol distributor, let's just say it's a tad more profitable than, say, being able to print your own money.

What makes my buddy's success even more exasperating for me is that he wanted me to be his partner after high school. But no, not me. I had to go to college and be the "smart" guy. Despite our economic disparity we've managed to stay pals.

So I asked him, "What do you suppose is the ratio of tangible vs intangible assets for say Amazon.com or Yahoo or even Microsoft?"

He looked annoyed now. "Alright, techno-nerd, maybe you have a point with those cyber companies but what about in the brick and mortar world?"

"Go ahead and name a company," I challenged.

"Starbucks," he said, with an air of victory.

"Okay, they have lots of prime real estate as well as equipment, inventory and cash. But what do you think is worth more to them: these tangible assets or their customer traffic? Or how about the ideas for leveraging that traffic in order to launch nearly intangible products like the latest obscure coffee concoctions they dream-up. Or the ability for customers to make their own CDs with the new Hear Music kiosks or the wireless high speed Internet connectivity? Isn't Starbucks really selling an experience, ideas for a cool new lifestyle, a place where people can influence and be influenced? Isn't it more about the "experience" than just the coffee?"

"Alright, alright. Coffee's for wimps anyway. Have a beer," Mike goaded me as he handed me a Budweiser long neck. He still knew how to win an argument.

Carving Out a Piece of Your Life

Maybe you're like Mike. Not yet ready to believe that the age of market share has past. Perhaps you think that it's all about mind share. That is how aware people are of your company, product or service.

Let me remind you that Starbucks isn't vying for more of the coffee market. Nor do they care if you remember their name. As long as you dig the "experience" in the store. As long as you and your friends like to meet and hang out there. That's what they're really after. When that happens they've won more than a greater share of the coffee market. They've gone beyond raising their top-of mind awareness. They're infiltrated your life. They have literally motivated you to carve out a piece of your life for them. They've gained greater heartshare.

Today, winning "share of heart" is far more critical than winning share of market or share of mind. "Market share" has been described as the proportion of industry sales that is controlled by a company. "Mind share" on the other hand is a measure of how people perceive the product, service or company as compared to the competition.

"HeartShare" is the measure of the extent to which we make ourselves more desirable to the people that are most critical to our success. Not by the quality or even the economic value of the products or services but rather in the "way" we provide them. Market share focuses on the size of the market. Mind share focuses on the perception of the brand. Heartshare focuses on the intangibles in the relationship.

HeartShare will help you to leverage your must valuable assets and become more desirable to those in your sphere of influence. Gaining greater heartshare will allow you to build better relationships as well as improve business performance.

Definitions:

"marketshare" - the measure of industry sales of a particular type of product or service which is controlled by a company.

"mindshare" - the measure of how people perceive a product, service or company as compared to the competition.

"heartshare" - the measure of growth, value and influence that our "intangible assets" produce for those in their sphere of influence.

How Sweet It Is

I remember Jackie Gleason in the early days of television opening his show with the one-liner, “How sweet it is.” Gleason had a difficult life and our country was going through a difficult time. Everything was clearly not sweet. But I think just saying “how sweet it is” was kind of a bittersweet encouragement to himself and the viewing audience. Ironic, but not cynical.

Winning a greater share of heart is just part of improving our condition and the condition of those around us. This must emanate from the heart just like Gleason’s “how sweet it is.”

Nearly every business person wants to achieve a better condition and continued growth - economic, social, and career advancement. These certainly make life more “sweet.” Peter Drucker said in his book *The Essential Drucker*, "It is not necessary for a business to grow bigger, but it is necessary that it constantly grow better.” Yet becoming “better” in this society is more than simply just a better product, increased sales and more productive workers.

Farewell, Old Guard

Whether my old pal Mike from Jersey believes it or not, there is a revolution in business today. The old way of doing things is passing into the dark mist of history. It used to be that you created a product or service that was needed or desired, obtained sufficient financing, recruited a great team, cranked-up your marketing machine and eventually you could grow to become a leader in your industry. That is until some smarter competitor produced a superior performing widget, secured better financing, stole some of your people or out-marketed you, thereby knocking you off your high horse.

Not anymore.

Don't believe me? Consider this: just recently, Bill Ford, president of Ford Motor Company and great grandson of founder Henry Ford said: "The business model that sustained us for decades is no longer sufficient to maintain profitability." Think about that for a minute. Here is the son of one of the "fathers of the industrial revolution" telling us that their business model no longer works. That's kind of heavy.

Product marketing, recruitment and financing are no longer the "sacred cows" of business success. They've been successfully toppled.

Product Marketing

Just because a product or service is "better" in no way guarantees its success in the market. In fact our friend Seth Godin, author and marketing guru says in his book, *The Purple Cow*, "Very good products and services are very bad!" Why? Because while we are focusing on how marvelous our products have become, the market has changed and often so radically that your nifty little product has not only lost demand, it has quite likely become irrelevant! Marketers today must focus on creating the *next* generation of products and services before their first generation ever hits the street. But often times we fall madly in love with our product line. This is a surefire approach to getting our clients to fall "out of love" with our company. Faster product and service turnover is a requirement of success in this blindingly fast, whim-sensitive culture.

Advertising Misses the Mark

Traditional advertising misses the mark as well. Frank Woolworth, America's first discount-retailer, and John Wanamaker, the father of the department store—both complained that they knew half of their advertising budget was wasted, but didn't know which half. As advertising starts to climb out of its recent slump, the answer to their problem is easier to find as the real effects of advertising become more measurable. But that is exposing another, potentially more horrible truth for the $1 trillion advertising and marketing industry: in some cases, it can be a lot more than half of the client's budget that is going down the drain. This is primarily because customers are just not motivated by advertising anymore. I believe we are living in a unique time in history. I believe that this is the age of heartshare.

Traditional Financing

While every enterprise must have some kind of basic financial foundation, today traditional financing is less important than ever before in history. Consider some of the recent start-ups that have grown into multi-million or billion dollar ventures with little or no traditional financing:

- Skype started with less than $10,000 in capital and recently sold to E-bay for 2.6 billion.
- Airborne Health with only 18 employees, posted $150 million in sales for 4673 percent growth in the last 3 years.
- Digital Lifestyle Outfitters, makers of i-pod accessories reached $84 million in sales after having been in business only 26 months!

All of these companies took risks. They were funded by immediate and astronomically growth not by a bunch of bankers with purse-strings and their greedy hands in every pie. I believe that self-funding ventures will become the standard for business growth in the future. Traditional financing and budgeting leads to waste. Like the old guard concept of, "it's in the budget, then we need to spend it or they will cut the budget next year." This is the kind of thinking that has created the 10 trillion dollar economic deficit that our generation faces.

Recruitment

Building a world-class corporate team has always been the aim of every great company. For years, Ford Motor Company had one of the lowest employee turnovers in their industry. For decades, loyal workers toiled for "mother company" in plants all over the Midwest. That is until the auto industry began to enter the world of collaboration and business alliances. Today it would be difficult to count how many different automotive companies take part in the design and manufacturing of most Japanese automobiles. In fact many of those cars are designed and made in collaboration with competitors. That's right, *competitors* actually cooperating.

If this is so effective for the global auto makers, why would it not work for small organizations like yours and mine? Because of *fear*. Many are afraid that their competitors will learn too much about us and use it to "beat us on the street." Many are afraid that our best employees will learn too much and defect to the competition. How foolish! What was stopping them from doing that very thing in the first place?

I remember people laughing at me many years ago when I said on live national radio that our corporate world is dying and that in less than a decade over seventy percent of the workforce will be free agents. I seemed to provoke so much anger that the calls flooded in and the CBS program manager called me and gave a good dressing-down. This is now very obviously happening, and that program manager is a free agent.

The watchwords of sustained growth in business today has been transformed from better product marketing, recruitment and financing to collaboration, risk-taking and blind fast product turnover, and winning the hearts of the customer. These have become the intangible variables that coalesce to permit organizations today to secure a more solid footing in the marketplace. They are the intangibles of winning greater heartshare.

The Intangibles of Heartshare

You may be reading this now and think, "You know Mark that sounds fine for big enterprises and institutions like Ford Motor Company but I'm just a little guy." Then let me tell you about Jeff, the clerk at the cleaners right here in our home town. Jeff runs the counter. That is to say he is responsible for taking your clothes, tagging them and getting them to the cleaning people in back of the store. When you return to pick them-up he must then take your money and return your cleaned clothes. Pretty simple job really. I wouldn't expect much rapport or interaction in that scenario. But Jeff goes far beyond simply performing these tasks. He always greets me by name. He has the clothes ready when he sees my car pull up. He makes sure that collar stays are inserted, he offers to put them in my car, he makes eye contact (which in itself is rare these days), he asks me SINCERELY about how my day is going and he is ALWAYS cheerful. My wife sometimes goes to the dry cleaners just to get an "uplift" in her day. I know that Jeff must have some difficult days like everyone else but one would never know it. You would think Jeff would be disinterested in this job. After all he's just doing it to earn a few dollars. You see Jeff is in medical school, studying to be a surgeon. Doesn't he have more important things to do than these menial tasks? All I can say is that if I ever need a surgeon, I hope I get someone like Jeff. If he goes out of his way to make my visit to the dry cleaners this memorable, how would he treat me as a patient? Imagine if your customers felt that way about dealing with you or your employees. That is what heartshare is all about.

Personal Action Plan

- How can you create an "experience" for customers in your business?
- What companies or organizations can you form alliances with?
- How can you incorporate social responsibility into your business?
- What next generation of products or services can you foresee emerging in your industry? What can you do now to be preparing for this emergence?
- What intangibles can you incorporate into your corporate culture that will leverage the power of heartshare?

Rule #10:

Collaborate Rather Than Compete

Corporate America is Dying!

My father and grandfathers worked for the same company for 20, 30, even 40 years. Generations of sons and daughters toiled their entire professional lives under the protective arms of the Company. Now, it's more likely each of us will outlive any organization that we work for. The shift has snuck up on us. We turned our head for a moment, and when we looked back, Corporate America was dying.

It is the result of a powerful force that has emerged in our society. Not a company or a new technology or even a new industry. It is the evolution of workers themselves. For the first time in history, there are more workers operating as "free agents" than there are people working for Corporate America. Fortune 500 companies no longer form the bedrock of our workforce.

The evolution has been rapid and decisive. It has occurred for a number of reasons. First, the social contract of job security has long been broken. Jobs are no longer sacrosanct at Fortune 500 companies. One day these firms are in expansion mode and the next they're laying off 35,000 workers. Second, e-commerce and automation technologies have leveled the playing field so that smaller companies with less people could provide the same benefits as larger multi-national firms. This resulted in corporate re-structuring and downsizing. The infiltration of foreign business services and outsourcing has quickened the pace of the demise. You would be hard pressed to call the customer service department of any large firm today and not end up talking with a representative from Singapore, the Philippines or India. In the last few years, thousands of these jobs have been exported due to economic efficiency. The loyalty/security pact of the previous five decades has been broken, as in the mid-nineties IBM broke its "full employment policy" by reducing its payroll by a whopping 120,000 employees. In this century, being loyal to a company does not guarantee job security.

What Does The Future Hold?

Today the largest private employer in America is not Ford, General Motors, or even Microsoft. It's Milwaukee's Manpower Inc., a temporary help agency with over 1,100 offices throughout the United States employing over a million workers. Temporary staffing has grown from a $1 billion industry to more than $80 billion while employing over ten million temps nationwide. It is estimated that there are over 33 million solo, self-employed workers. And there is an emergence of micro businesses, small businesses employing just two or three people to drive particular initiatives on either a full or part time basis. In fact, more than half of today's companies have fewer than five employees! Don't look to our government to reconcile this societal evolution. They're a full century behind. The Bureau of Labor and Statistics still divides all workers into two categories: farm and non-farm. Figure that out.

The work ethic of free agent entrepreneurs is considerably different than corporate employees. These entrepreneurs crave, freedom, control, security, and loyalty—the very job benefits lacking in corporate America. Today free agents come in a variety of forms: entrepreneurs, service providers, independent contractors, consultants, advisors, 1099ers, hired guns, nomads, etc. But their focus is on producing a measurable result for an organization rather than performing a specific role within it. Free agents tend to provide a higher return on investment for organizations because of their accountability to themselves rather than to a hierarchy.

Freedom, Control and Security

Freedom is the ability to exercise one's own will. Within the corporate cocoon freedom takes on the meaning which the company as a whole projects. Some companies smother their employees in affection; others try to purchase individual freedom with stock options and incentives. Free agents can choose to follow their own work ethic. This extends not only to what they believe, what they do and where they do it but also *when* they do it. Free agents have succeeded in melding work time with home time. Gone is the Monday through Friday 9am to 5pm ritual. Today, workers balance a full time home life with a full time work life, and the once-distinct spheres overlap. For years, organizational psychologists have preached that employers need to foster a "balanced" life approach to their employees. But free agents can practice a "blended lifestyle" which is ultimately more productive, appealing and engaging.

In the past, work-life in corporate America was about lining up behind the company culture and philosophy. Free agents can control their own destiny. Consequently, they develop vertical skills in areas which they desire to excel. They build relationships with those that match their business culture and paradigm. They focus on selling insight, talent, expertise, ideas, creativity and solutions rather than just performing tasks. They realize that what matters in the course of a day is what is accomplished not how many hours are worked.

The last decade has been one of prosperity, while the next decades loom uncertainly. Members of corporate America had job security, but that prospect is diminishing. While a high standard of living has flowed down to middle class pockets, many members of corporate America do not feel that their lives have improved. This dichotomy has altered our expectations of comfort and prosperity. People are looking forward to more than just a comfortable retirement after four or five decades of work. People are realizing that it's not good enough to work to make money and survive. They desire to work to make *meaning* for themselves and their families.

All of this creates a natural environment for leveraging *intangibles*.

Fostering the Free Agent Model

Free agents have greater control over their finances and personal satisfaction. For one thing, loyalty does not run up and down an organizational chart in a free agent relationship. It runs from side-to-side in allegiance to clients, colleagues, teams, projects, vendors and industries. In this sense, free agents are far more accountable and loyal than company men and women. Companies can also afford to be more loyal to free agents because they lack the overhead that employees bring. Just hearing the words, "Workers Comp" speaks volumes on this subject to many small business owners that have found themselves unable to grow or even meet their financial obligations because of the ever-increasing cost of employing a workforce in the traditional manner. With the free-agent structure, when employed ethically and legally, both partners benefit because while vertical loyalty within an organization is dependent on one connection (boss and employee) this new horizontal loyalty depends on many connections. Often in a free agent relationship, compensation is structured with the goal of winning greater dependability, higher production and more accountability. This creates *attraction* from both perspectives. It also inspires growth. In this way free agents can improve capability and capacity more quickly. In addition, free agents are able to become specialists. This makes them far more valuable to their client/employers as well as viable to other client/employers. The free agent mentality is symbiotic and smooth for both client/employer as well as the free agent themselves.

I'm certain that we'll the free agent philosophy infiltrate every industry, profession and area of expertise. Those who are most prepared for this transition will position themselves to win the greatest share of market, mind and heart—both as a client/employer of free agents as well as a free agent themselves. I encourage even the smallest business to employ the free agent mentality. This might mean identifying areas requiring specialists in your business. This could be in the production process or the delivery or the acquisition. Think about what and who you can out-source and with whom you may be able to collaborate. Some might ask: "what if I turn my employees into free agents and they try to become my competitors?" Don't let this irrational fear stop you from developing the free-agent approach to growing your business. Try to develop a non-competitive, cooperative relationship with at least one or more members and test the concept. You'll have to make some adjustments as you go, but I assure you the free agent approach is the fastest, easiest way to maximize efficiency, innovation and growth.

Technological Collaboration

Collaboration can also occur with other companies outside the organization— directly with supplier, client or even competitor. Siemens, the global communications company, announced in 2004 that it would cooperate with its biggest rivals, Motorola and Ericsson, to achieve the goal of developing a standard for "push-to-talk" technology. Why would these competitors cooperate on such a mission-critical technology? Aren't they afraid that one competitor might hold back a key ingredient? Or that one competitor might use information gained to try to damage or eliminate the other competitor once and for all?

Not at all! They have far bigger fish to fry, as my grandfather was fond of saying. Push-to-talk allows handsets to be used like walkie-talkies—a feature mobile phone operators believe will significantly increase their revenues by encouraging users to talk more. Apparently, the three companies will conduct tests to make their technologies totally compatible with each other, enabling customers of different operators to talk to one another—an essential development if push-to-talk is to penetrate the mass market. Do you think this technological collaboration will have a negative or positive effect on the revenues and client satisfaction of each player? Do you think that this will increase or decrease the attraction of each of these players? I know what I think: I'm persuaded this collaboration could literally revolutionize the telecommunications industry making Ericsson, Siemens and Motorola the only games in town.

Co-opetition

Many would say that our entire free-economy system is built on the foundation of competition. Competition drives the supply and demand curve, is the catalyst in pricing models and the fuel for innovation. I have no argument—I love competition!

But cooperation and collaboration with our competitors is equally as valuable. *Co-opetition*, a book by Adam Brandenburger and Barry Nalebuff of Yale Business Management School, makes a powerful case that under specific circumstances there is greater value in cooperating with certain customers, suppliers and even competitors instead of doing battle. The central concept: we can create complementary product or service relationships that allow products and services to become more important when purchased *together* rather than separately. This relationship results in a reduction of marketing costs and ultimately in an increase in market share, client loyalty and even brand value. Using game theory, the authors demonstrate how complementary related products can lead to expansion of the market and the formation of new business relationships.

In order to increase our *attraction,* we must seek out those partners that compliment our business. A compliment is a product or service that makes any other product or service more attractive. The classic example of compliments is computer hardware and software. Faster hardware prompts people to upgrade. Powerful software motivates people to buy faster hardware. E.g.,Windows and Pentium chips.

I needed to make color copies of a report so I went to the standard: Kinko's. We all know Kinko's as a reliable, convenient, cost effective place to get your reports printed, copied and bound. As I pulled in the parking lot, I watched a group of sign-installers taking down the old Kinko's sign and replacing it with a new one: FedEx Kinko's. Prior to acquiring Kinko's, FedEx spent millions on testing the concept of combining locations. The test was so successful that FedEx eventually bought Kinko's—a move that made a great deal of business sense. If you are going to a store to design, develop, print and copy business or personal communication material, doesn't it make sense that you will want to *ship* those materials somewhere? For FedEx, collaborating with Kinko's turned-out to be a tremendous windfall.

Discovering "Complementors" is about finding shifting perspective: instead of fighting over how to slice up the pie, find a way to make the pie bigger. So how do we identify competitors and complementors? A player is a complementor if customers value your product more when they have the other player's product than when they have your product alone. Customers value Kinko's more now that FedEx is located directly inside the Kinko's location. What used to take visiting two locations now takes one visit. This makes things smoother for the customer and increases value for both partners.

A player is a *competitor* if customers value your product *less* when they have the other player's product than when they have your product alone. Coca-Cola and Pepsi-Cola—either you like one or the other. No one goes into a convenience store and orders a Coke and a Pepsi at the same time. One is valued in *exclusion* of the other.

Here are some typical partners engaged in successful complementary marketing relationships:

- Disney and McDonald's
- Universal and Burger King
- Sears and All-State
- Visa and American Airlines
- Oscar Meyer Hot Dogs and Gulden's Mustard

Vendor Supplier Collaboration

The above examples represent collaborative relationships at the end of the supply chain. That is to say, the collaboration occurs in the arena where marketers cooperate to increase the potential customer or share opportunity for each player. Collaboration can also be used at the beginning of the supply chain to significantly reduce the cost of manufacturing, development or delivery. Suppliers, vendors and end-users can collaborate on technology, applications, processes in the supply chain in order to make themselves more competitive and attractive as an industry.

Ed Marien, director of logistics and transportation management programs at the University of Wisconsin School of Business, has made a career out of studying collaborative strategies. He said in an interview with *Supply Chain Brain*, an industry publication, that "collaborative alliances are a means of sharing strengths." He cites the company Federal-Mogul, a piston maker for the automotive industry that is using its buying power to purchase sheet metal for many of its suppliers at a lower cost than they could negotiate alone. How about process collaboration? Consider Bridgestone/Firestone, which began mounting its tires on wheels at the request of automotive assemblers. As is happening in many cases, this activity has been spun off into a whole new business unit that now is mounting not only its own tires but also those of Bridgestone's competitors. That this unit has become one of the company's fastest-growing and most profitable divisions illustrates how alliances can lead companies to develop core strengths they did not previously have.

Strategic Alliances

The number of strategic alliances in the U.S. is surging. More than 20,000 new alliances were formed in just the last 4 years, compared with 5100 between 1980 and 1987 and 750 during the 1970s—all this according to Keeley, Kuenn & Reid, a Chicago based law firm with government relations affiliates in Washington, D.C.

Nearly 6 percent of the revenue generated from the top 1000 U.S. firms now comes from alliances, a fourfold increase since 1987. Alliances generally achieve a higher return on investment (seventeen percent) than U.S. industry in general (eleven percent). The higher return is a direct result of leveraging partners' resources and assets, requiring lower investment to produce greater incremental returns. Alliances also showed a greater success rate (sixty percent) than outright acquisitions (fifty percent success) or venture capital arrangements (twenty-five percent success).

Types of Alliances

There are many types of strategic alliances. Basic types include:

- Licensing technology or intellectual property
- Joint research and product development
- Cross-purchase agreements
- Manufacturing arrangements
- Sales/Cross marketing collaboration

How to Select an Alliance Partner

These collaborative strategies can transform your business, help you capture greater market share, improve your profitability, or even help you start a new business and reduce your financial risk in this difficult economy. But they're just nice ideas until we put them into action.

1. Develop a profile of potential partners.
2. Identify at least five non-competitive partners that you can collaborate with and create a pre-approach plan.
3. Pick only the very best people in each area.
4. Be very selective Do NOT compromise on values or philosophy.
5. Ensure that there is mutual benefit. A one sided relationship will only breed resentment and contempt.

How to Put Alliance and Affiliate Programs into Action

Some of the specific things that you can do to make alliances more effective:

- **Informational Alliance Marketing**
  Write a newsletter that can be branded as coming from the partner. This allows each partner access to the other's sphere of influence. It is important that valuable information is communicated in the newsletter. If this is merely a sales pitch, it will not be nearly as effective.

- **Train Affiliates**
  Write a sales training manual with questions to ask prospects, and fact/benefit charts. This is a great way of preparing partners by offering the information necessary to endorse your product or service. The more prepared your partners are, the more effective they will be positioning your product or service for the customer. I might even suggest holding some formal training sessions hosted by one partner for the others. Each

partner could take turns being the trainer. This creates continuity and rapport as well as mutual education.

- **Create an Ideation Session**
  About 15 years ago I had the great fortune of working with the American Express Company as a consultant, specifically retained to provide soft enhancements for their retail credit card services. We held what we called "ideation sessions." These were brainstorming meetings where we came up with all kinds of wild ideas and discussed their merit. I traveled to New York two or three times per month for nearly a year and we would hold up in what was once World Trade Tower One and kick around all kinds of programs. We finally stumbled upon the "Buyers Assurance Program" which became the "Big Daddy" of all credit card enhancements. It essentially doubled the warranty of any product purchased with an American Express Card. We thought, "let's outsource everything!" We found an insurance company to carry the risk, a national service provider to handle exchanges and repairs, a customer service company to handle the telephone calls and a mail center to handle the response. Everyone got a little piece of the pie and AMEX just skimmed the cream off the top. Sometimes it is the process of discovery that is most valuable in alliance and affiliate marketing. Great ideas often need the right environment and enough time to be born. How about getting your partners together and letting the sparks fly. Maybe you'll create a hybrid solution, a revolutionary product or new service.

- **Mutual Marketing Affiliations**
  You can also provide ad designs that partners can brand as their own. In this way you will create an effective ad, then let any affiliate stamp their logo on it and run it in

selected media. This is similar to the co-op advertising concept but broadens the appeal for both partners. It also helps both partners get a bigger bang for their advertising dollar. We often see this in automobile business. Auto manufacturers create fabulous advertising for dealers to use. Dealers then tag their name to these print ads, TV commercials and radio spots, and they run them in their local area. The exceptional production quality adds credibility to the message and ad effectiveness soars. Think about how you could do this in your business. Could you benefit from tagging your affiliates to your ads? How about the reverse?

- **Seamless Strategies**
  Create exclusive offers that are smooth and seamless for your partner's clients. These can be offered in a variety of forms. Take for example QuickBook's resource site. If you want to order checks or envelopes you can do it seamlessly on the QuickBooks Web site. But you never even realize that you are actually purchasing from another company until the shipment arrives. Who cares? You're happy to know that the checks and envelopes you purchased were compatible with QuickBooks and it was fast, easy and cheap. You'd probably do it again when you ran out. How could you apply this to your business?

- **Web Alliances**
  Alliances are particularly effective for Internet media. How about actually building Web sites for affiliates? This is a very powerful way to ensure that your host's clients are locked into your solution. We can essentially build a captive audience on the Web yet branded as the host's site. Visitors are not at all aware that you are the beneficiary of their purchases. In fact they are not even aware that they are on another Web site since it

looks the same as the host site. This is similar to the QuickBooks example but as the beneficiary you make the investment in building a Web site for the host.

- **Free Goods**
  Create a free introductory sample only for your partner's clients. These can be marketed via brick and mortar as well as on the Internet. The free sample is a great way to introduce your product or service to what would otherwise be a lost prospect. This is made even more valuable by the fact that the person receiving the free goods has a predisposition to be interested in your product or service by the relationship with your affiliate.

- **Super Referrers**
  How about using the affiliate strategy to build a network of "Super Referrers?" I know a plastic surgeon that helped to recruit the most powerful potential influencers in her community and make them super referrers. She asked the local day spa, massage therapist, nail solon, beauty center, cosmetics retailer and more to donate samples and discount coupons. Then she partnered with a gift basket company and created a beautiful gift basket including all kinds of free samples donated by her new partners. She then gave this basket to all of her new patients. Of course they were thrilled since the basket and its massive contents were valued at over $1000! The patients couldn't wait to visit all of the partners and use their coupons. This obviously helped the doctor's partners increase their business while at the same time helping the doctor ensure all of her partners exclusively refer to her. Everyone wins.

- **Targeted Discounts**
  Offer a discount coupon to a special subgroup of your partner's clients in order to gain access to a highly targeted audience. HP and Staples office supplies has successfully run this type of program where Staples gives a $50 gift certificate to every customer but it can *only* be used by teachers. The hope of course is that these folks will give their coupons to teachers, the teachers will patron Staples, and become regular customers. But additionally, offering such a discount to teachers wins a little thing called heartshare.

- **Symbiosis**
  Seen the Disney/Pixar film *Finding Nemo*? Nemo is a clown fish, which depend upon the sea anemone to protect them. While the anemone is deadly to all other sea life, the clown fish is resistant to its venom. On the other hand, the beautiful colors of the clown fish attract sea life for anemone to sting and devour. The clown fish then gets the leftovers. That's what naturalists call *symbiosis*.

  Many companies have adopted this type of symbiotic relationship. Have you walked into the grocery store lately and been surprised to see a Starbucks or a branch of the post office or your bank's ATM machines sitting between the canned goods and the paper towel aisle? These are also symbiotic relationships. Who can you symbiotically partner with?

Affiliates, Alliances and Collaboration

In the world of business relationships, two heads are better than one, and collaboration is the buzz word of our day. There are several types of collaboration, including affiliates, alliances and joint ventures, and the best types of collaboration are those that both reduce costs while creating an additional income stream.

The Joint Venture

A Joint Venture is where two or more businesses share resources to create profitable new income opportunities, which otherwise would be too costly for only one of the businesses to achieve on their own. This structure can be found anywhere, but many particular industries seem to be practicing this type of collaboration today. An example would be the Wal-Mart Super Center. When you walk into a Wal-Mart Super Center you see clothes, furniture, groceries, electronics, movies, etc. Imagine with all the different categories what it takes to merchandise this store. In reality Wal-Mart's products are merchandised through a joint venture with the manufacturers of the products they sell. In the end both Wal-Mart and the manufacturers are profiting. Various brands can showcase their products and sell them, and Wal-Mart earns a portion of the sale for allowing them the use of their storefronts. They also save money on the need for specialized labor and merchandising costs. Wal-Mart knows how to outsource. This is truly a 'win-win' collaborative relationship.

Business within a Business

Even more creative is the store within a store concept. An outlet store inside the larger retailers. Inside a local grocery store stands a video arcade, a Bank of America, a hair salon, and a Starbucks. The partnership works for all: parents come to the grocery to shop, and they leave their kids to play video games and pick them up when they are finished. They can do their banking, get a haircut, have a coffee or a snack. This lowers costs, provides rental income, increases convenience and creates a better customer experience.

> **Cross Marketing Collaboration**
> The consumer electronics company, Bang and Olfsen, and Bentley automotive recently created a successful collaborative promotion. Bang and Olfsen wanted to preview their newest line of $5,000 audiophile speakers and Bentley wanted to introduce their latest sports coupe. So they shared customer lists in several key cities and created an event so that customers could experience both new products in a comfortable casual environment. They sponsored "listening parties" at several local high-end audio retailers. Clients were picked-up in these beautiful new Bentley motorcars and whisked to the party to listen to the new speakers. They sold several hundred speakers in just a few weeks and more than a dozen cars. The cost was next to nothing.

This manner of collaboration literally smashes the traditional concept of supplier, vendor and competitive relationships. The line between partner, competitor and supplier is blurred. And that's good for everybody.

Personal Action Plan

- Think about your own business life. Are you stuck in the corporate mentality? Even if you are employed by a large organization, you may be able to employ segments of the free agent mentality. Ask yourself:
    - How can you use the "free agent mentality" to bring efficiencies to your work?
    - If you're an employer, how could you increase productivity and reduce overhead by employing free agents?
    - If you're an employee, how could you deliver greater production to your employer and increase your earning capacity by utilizing the above free agent infrastructure?

- Who are some "complementors" in your product, service or industry category? What can you do to build cooperative relationships with them?
- Who are good complementors for your business? As a business advisor, good complementors for me are attorneys, CPA's, designers, Internet professionals, computer consultants, training companies, TV and radio stations, magazines, newspapers, printers, and more.
- Brainstorm a list of 5 to 10 complementary businesses.
- Then make a list of specific contacts within those categories that could currently be utilized. First see what you can do to help them. Then watch the magic of co-*opetition* unfold!
    - How to structure the alliance to ensure that both parties benefit
    - Integrate alliance efforts into your overall marketing plan
    - Use an alliance to look ten times bigger than you already are
    - Use affiliates to overcome price objections
    - Numerous case studies and the examples of success stories

Rule #11:

Who We Are is More Important than What We Do

Character

It has been said that one's "character" is displayed by what he does when no one is watching. Indeed, character is "who we are – defined." And it is composed of the values we adhere to, extending beyond a trait that defines a person's temperament or disposition.

In the twenty-first century marketing arena, character or "who we are" is more important than ever, and I believe that character is far more important than what we do or say about our company, product or service.

Character is the *evidence* of our most persuasive claims.

As products and services are becoming more homogeneous, as differentiating oneself is becoming more and more difficult, and as competition in every industry and profession accelerates daily, *character* may be the deciding factor in *attracting* better clients, more committed team members, and healthier relationships.

There are a number of intangible traits that define "who we are" or "who our company is." Some of the most critical are: Integrity, Vision, Enthusiasm, Selflessness. When the perception of these intangibles holds a positive position in the minds of others, we are said to have "strong character," and our company a positive reputation. This certainly builds attraction, as people are drawn to a person or a company with strong character. Thus, we are free from the burden of needing to chase clients or forcefully pursue relationships. Those having a strong character are magnetic, drawing to themselves the right circumstances, relationships, and resources.

Integrity

When we think of the greatest military leaders of all time, we think of Patton, Eisenhower, and MacArthur. The name George C. Marshall has faded into the mist. However, Marshall was the leader that made it possible for these men to dominate the history books. Marshall was the boss of each: the Chief of Staff of the United States Armed Forces during World War II. He forfeited his chance to go down in history as the hero of the war and gave up the chance to position himself as a leading candidate for the Presidency.

In late 1943, at the height of World War II, Marshall had convinced both President Roosevelt and Winston Churchill that the best way to turn the tide of the war was to plan a cross-channel attack on Germany via France. The only question was who would lead the operation? Roosevelt knew that Marshall wanted to be the commander of the D-Day invasion. It would virtually guarantee Marshall's place in history. Yet just as Roosevelt knew that Marshall deserved this honor, he also was aware that the man was so humble he would never ask for the job. The President's problem was that he felt that Marshall was more greatly needed as the high commander of the entire war effort than he was as leader of the D-Day invasion.

So what did the President do? Like any good politician he hedged his bet. He sent a message to Marshall telling him that if the general wanted the position then he just needed to ask for it. What was Marshall's reply? He sent a one line message back to Roosevelt saying:

"I will serve wherever you order me, Mr. President."

In the end, the Normandy invasion, a virtual guarantee of glory, slipped from the hands of Marshall into those of Eisenhower who used it to make his successful play for the Presidency. However Marshall demonstrated his integrity by having the courage and conviction to make the "right decision" for the country. Marshall knew that in fact he was more greatly needed in the role of overseer for the entire war effort than he was as D-Day invasion commander. Later, when asked why he made such a decision, he said, "The issue was just too great for personal feelings to be considered."

This is the kind of integrity that creates attraction. While many of today's business leaders are shifting blame, slamming competitors and whining about fair treatment, those with integrity are willing to tell the truth, make sacrifices, do the right thing and do it consistently. Imagine the reputation your company can build in a marketplace hungry for products, services, companies and people with integrity.

Vision

Go to any business retreat or management conference and you'll hear one word more than any other: vision. There's a lot of discussion today about vision, mission and goals. I see many companies investing loads of time, money and effort in coming up with their "mission statement." Usually this is a few inspiring sentences that are placed on plaques to hang on the wall or printed on the back of business cards or put on the company Web site. With few exceptions, despite the good intentions, this often amounts to a big waste of time.

Few of these mission statements accomplish what they intend: to create attraction in the marketplace, and to motivate team members. After a month (or sooner), not even the CEO, let alone clients or employees, can remember the mission statement that too so much time to craft.

So does this mean establishing a mission for your company is a useless task?

Not necessarily. Yet in order to make mission planning a valuable tool we must first understand what a *mission* is. In short, a mission is a course of action that a company decides to pursue. It is the road they will travel in order to ensure they arrive at their ultimate destination. It is their plan for achieving their vision. A mission is not something we *say*, it is something we *do*. It is the *reason* for the decisions we make.

Leaders of companies often make the mistake of developing their mission in the wrong way, by trying to figure out what their mission is before they decide where they want to go. Imagine trying to do this when going on a trip. Can you really plan how you're going to get somewhere if you don't know where it is you want to end up?

In Lewis Caroll's fantastical adventure, *Alice in Wonderland*, Alice approaches the Cheshire cat for help. Having approached a fork in the road, she asks:

> *"Would you tell me, please, which way I ought to go from here?" asked Alice.*

"That depends a good deal on where you want to get to," said the Cat.

"I don't much care where," said Alice.

"Then it doesn't matter which way you go," said the Cat.

As leaders, we see our employees going in different directions. Or we see that we're unable to maintain a consistent level of performance. Or we see clients that perceive us as no different than the competition. This directionless mode is due most often to a lack of certainty regarding where precisely where it is we want to go. The desire to be profitable and efficient is not a goal, or a path, just as good intentions is not a strategy.

Developing a mission is quite impossible until we establish a vision of our destination. We must be able to see it, feel it, smell it and taste it.

This cannot be accomplished solely by the marketing department or a consulting firm. While the vision should be shared by many, it must be owned by and burning in the heart of the leaders of the company. Unless the CEO and his or her leadership team are totally driven by their vision, it will be meaningless in the arms of their employees. As useless as a plaque on the wall.

Great leaders have in common the ability to dream big dreams and create a powerful vision of the future. They seem to have the ability to imagine an ideal future well in advance of creating it. It is this that creates attraction both internally and eternally.

Our vision is an imaginary creation of the ideal life we would like to live, *in every respect*. We create it as an expression of the *values* that we hold most dear. Brian Tracy says, "From the very day that you develop a clear vision for who you are and where you are going in life, you begin to become a superior person, and soon you begin to accomplish superior results."

Here's some advice on how you can develop a clear vision for your company that will help to drive a sense of purpose, improve performance and create greater attraction.

1. Let your mind float freely. One of the great secrets of success is to "dream big dreams." Imagine that you have no limitations on what you can be, have, or do. Imagine for the moment that you have all of the resources that you would ever need to achieve the highest goals to which you could ever aspire. Imagine you have all the time, money, people, contacts and intelligence that you could ask for to become everything that you could ever become. Power can be generated by a person who communicates a compelling vision of the future.

2. Create your ideal future. What would you like to be engraved on your head stone when you die? What would you like people to say about you? What great things would you like to accomplish? How will it change the world or improve people's lives in some way? What is it you would like to "give back" to our society your industry or profession? Since you attract into your life people and situations that are in harmony with the person you really are, what kind of attributes and qualities would you like to develop in yourself so that you can live the very best life you can imagine, surrounded by the kind of people you would most enjoy?

3. Make sure the vision is understood by everyone. John F. Kennedy did not live to see the achievement of his vision for NASA to put a man on the moon, but he set it in motion when he delivered his famous speech. The American people were no doubt moved by the *vision*. Initially, however, he received much opposition from Congress, due to the Cold War and the fear of technological failure. A team of legislators were sent to Cape Canaveral to determine whether the funding should be allocated for the project. Florida Senator George Smathers, a member of this team, toured the

facility. He slipped away from the group of dignitaries for a moment to get a drink of water, but became lost and found himself wandering the halls. The space was immaculate, sanitized, pristine. He came upon a women sweeping up and explained his situation to her. She seemed to know her way around the complex and quickly told him how to rejoin his party. Smathers, impressed with the women's knowledge, asked her, "What is it that you do here?" her answer: "I am part of a team helping to put a man on the moon and bring him back safely." Smathers went back to Washington in full support of the lunar project. He told his colleagues, "If the janitor at Cape Canaveral has this kind of sense of mission, what might the scientists and astronauts be like?"

4. Make the vision memorable. I recommend a practical exercise to develop your organizational vision: by following this plan you may be better assured that the vision statement you develop is a shared one. Plan an uninterrupted time to work on the vision with key team members. At this meeting, take an hour to explore your vision. Agree on a rough time frame of five to ten years. Ask people to think about the following questions: How do you want your organization to be different? What role do you want each department or team (for smaller companies each person) to play in your organization? What will success look like? Then ask each member to come up with a metaphor for your organization, and to draw a picture of success: "Our organization is like a mariachi band, all playing the same music together; or like a train, pulling important cargo and laying the track as we go." The value of metaphors is that people get to stretch their minds and experiment with different ways of thinking about what success means to them. Finally,

have everyone share their pictures of success with each other. One person should facilitate the discussion and help the group discuss what their various images mean and what they hope for. Look for areas of agreement, as well as moments of difference that emerge. The goal is to find language and imagery that your organization's members can relate to as their vision for success. By thinking *visually*, we can increase the chance that the vision will be memorable

5. Do not try to write a vision statement with a group. (Groups are great for many things, but writing is not one of them!). Ask one or two people to try drafting a vision statement based on the group's discussion, bring it back to the group, and revise it until you have something that your members can agree on and that your leaders share with enthusiasm.

Only when you have a clear, memorable vision of the future that everyone understands and feels enthusiastic about can you begin working on the mission or path that you will take. Following the vision are the steps to achieve it. A clear vision will allow you as a leader to propel your company forward. It will make creating marketing communication material easier than ever before. It will make daily decision making easier for every member of the organization. It will allow the organization to move initiatives forward with greater speed and agility. It will motivate a higher level of performance and commitment among your team. It will significantly differentiate "who you are" perceived to be in the market place. And all of this creates far greater *attraction*.

Enthusiasm

I'll never forget my first marketing consulting sale. We were eating lunch in Long Beach California. John Nethery, president of Dale

Carnegie Training in California, was listening intently to what I had to say. I showed him charts and graphs of projected response. I gave him a detailed explanation of the CPM (cost per thousand) of the advertising spots we would run. I even reviewed a PERT chart that I prepared showing him how the ads would role out. Finally I said, "So what do you think, John?"

Now John was a Good Ol' Arkansas boy. He leaned back in his chair, gave a little chuckle and looking at me over his glasses said with a thick drawl, "Well you know buddy-boy, I haven't the slightest idea what in the heck you've been talking about but I'll do it because *I like your enthusiasm*!"

John passed away a few years later, but before he did, I counted him as my mentor. He changed my life and he turned me into a Dale Carnegie instructor. I still miss him, but I'll never forget that lunch. To this day, whenever I'm trying to convince someone of an idea I just pour on a little more enthusiasm and I'm always amazed at the result. Dale Carnegie said in *How to Win Friends and Influence People*, that enthusiasm is the little known secret of success. John would have agreed.

While enthusiasm is an important component of attraction it must be *real.* Forced or phony enthusiasm is easily recognizable, and has long given sales a bad name. Nothing turns people off faster. But true, authentic enthusiasm is a contagious and effective means of creating attraction.

Emeril Lagasse is the best-known chef in America. How did it happen? "Emeril's vision and genuine enthusiasm has accounted for the phenomenal growth of the company," says Eric Linquest, Emeril's vice president and general manager. "We started the first restaurant with about 40 employees, and now we have 20 times that number. Believe me, Emeril has always known how to take advantage of every opportunity." The charismatic Emeril has been delighting audiences for years with his unrestrained approach to the joy of cooking on the Food Network show, *Emeril Live.* Even the dullest cooking chores can be exciting to watch when -- *Bam*! -- Emeril adds his personality. There is no doubt that Emeril's enthusiasm is real. He does what he likes to do best, and he involves his entire audience in his excitement. His ebullience is evident every time I watch him. Compare Emeril with other celebrity chefs like Wolfgang Puck, Nathalie Dupree and the late Julia Child: while they may have been accomplished in the culinary arts, they were not nearly as compelling, interesting or attractive. Emeril is a great example of rule # 11 in action. Truly, who Emeril *is* increases his level of attraction far more than what he *does*.

Sometimes it's not so much what we say but "how" we say it. And no one said it like the late Steve Irwin, the Crocodile Hunter. Who else could get millions excited about a beak-billed platypus? I had the pleasure of meeting Steve years ago and I can tell you that his enthusiasm is not only real and genuine, but that it was born out of personal experiences in his youth with all types of animals.

He truly cared for the plight of the world's wildlife. Irwin said his love affair with the beasts of the bush began on his sixth birthday when he received the birthday present that he always wanted—his very own scrub python! It was twelve feet long. So while most other children were opening cans of pet food for their cats or dogs, Steve was out catching fish and hunting rodents to feed to his crocodiles and snakes.

There was not a moment that Steve wasn't displaying his enthusiasm for these animals. On camera or off he was literally on fire for their way of life. Even the photo-stills that we see of Irwin in print ads, product endorsements and on Web sites show him with a surprised and delighted look on his face as he wrestled with a croc or held a python at bay. When I was last in Australia, I was told by many that they believed that Steve had done more for the country economically than the last two Prime Ministers had. There is no doubt that genuine enthusiasm has its rewards. Queensland Premier Peter Beattie's government nominated Irwin for Australian of the Year and he has built a billion dollar industry out of absolutely nothing. He created a product that is impossible to remove from himself. It's not so much what he does that has us sitting at the edge of our chair, it is who he is that engages us.

The fabulous thing about enthusiasm is that it is so easily transferable. While watching television recently, I came across the Crocodile Hunter battling some prehistoric-looking creature in the

Aussie brush. I thought, here's my old friend Steve Irwin, animal enthusiast, environmentalist and master marketer, dead and gone, yet his show is still in reruns.

But it wasn't a re-run. It was a new show, and was being narrated by Bindi, Steve and Terri's little daughter. She was articulate, interesting, and real. Another extension of the fabulous enterprise that Steve had built.

Not only does Bindi, all of nine years, host *The Crocodile Hunter*, but she has her own TV series on Discovery for Kids dubbed *Jungle Girl*, and she has released her first CD of music, along with a line of clothes for kids called "Bindi Wear." Now Steve's daughter has carried-on his enthusiasm. Even in death, his brand and enthusiasm is unstoppable.

Despite the controversy swirling around Irwin, he demonstrates the power of enthusiasm in creating positive and continuing attraction.

Selflessness

From our early days in school, when we first hear about evolution, and that catchphrase that's persisted through the years, "survival of the fittest," we begin to believe that the world is red in tooth and claw. That is, we must fight for what is ours, and the world is dog eat dog.

But Henry Stimson, Secretary of War during World War II, and a gentlemen versed in the strategies of war and the drive to be the fittest, said, "No one who is thinking of himself can rise to great heights."

We remain fascinated with those famous selfless individuals who have changed the world. People like Gandhi, Mother Teresa and Nelson Mandela. Their selfless actions created massive attraction. This type of character-based attraction, like integrity, vision and enthusiasm, can be implemented in a powerful and genuine way.

In his youth, Gandhi was a regular guy. In fact the name Gandhi means "grocer." Educated as a lawyer in England, he ultimately managed to lead his people to freedom from British rule by practicing nothing but selflessness. He never wavered in his unshakable belief in nonviolent protest and religious tolerance. When Muslim and Hindu compatriots committed acts of violence, whether against the British, or against each other, he fasted until the fighting ceased. Independence, when it came in 1947, was not a military victory, but a triumph of human will.

Mother Teresa taught at St. Mary's High School in Calcutta from 1931 to 1948. However the suffering and poverty she saw outside the convent made a profound impression on her. She asked for permission from her superiors to leave the school and devote herself to working with the destitute and dying in the slums of Calcutta. Although she did not have a single penny, she relied on Divine Providence, and began the first school for slum children without even a building. Her selflessness attracted volunteers and eventually financial support. By the '90s, there were over one million co-workers in more than 40 countries.

What would happen if we took the long view, overlooking confrontation in favor of a selflessness? If you really enacted such a philosophy, you've find yourself growing in attractiveness. In a society that focuses on gratifying ourselves, imagine the response we'd receive from clients, shareholders and team members if we became the only, the exclusive, business that acted from a model of selflessness!

Identity over Action

Mark Cuban has used his identity to create attraction. He is so committed to his team and the game that he has actually garnered more media attention than the players! This is more than simply team spirit. Nelson Mandela was imprisoned for 28 years and won the heart of his captors. Paul Newman gives one hundred percent of profits to charity. Bono has gone from being a regular rock star to an icon of philanthropy. You may call this a good marketing gimmick, but the sincerity of each of these is hard to doubt.

What does all this have to do with becoming more attractive and differentiating ourselves in the market? In the end people can see through all the hype. Our identity is built based on "truth." In order to build an identity for a product, service or company we must focus on obtaining highly visible, positive exposure with a message or promise that is custom-tailored to a highly exclusive and targeted audience. Think of Jaguar or Mercedes. Consumers will pay more for the promise underlying those brands. Volvo's implicit concern for safety has come to signify their image and brand. But the brand elements must be true to the identity. If Volvo began to compromise on their commitment to safety either in the product development, innovate safety features or even in the commitment to the "safety message" in their marketing, you would find a brand suddenly in the cold without an identity and without an audience. Volvo has won a significant share of heart by maintaining the perception that they are the safest vehicle on the road. Who they are—their identity—is far more important than what they do—their activity.

Personal Action Plan

- Chart out your vision.
- List your values. What of these would you like to change? Why? If you'd like to learn more about discovering values, visit www.markdeo.com/rulesofattraction for our values exercise.
- How would you like to ensure that these extend into your business?
- Who on your team does not hold values congruent with your own? They may need to leave.

Rule #12:

Create Standards and Systems that Nurture Growth

Black Bamboo

I spent a great deal of time in Japan during the '90s, and while there, I met an elderly gentleman who kept a beautiful bamboo garden in his yard. A neighbor to the home where I was staying, he was one of the few people that spoke English in the neighborhood, and we quickly became friends. One day, he offered me a walking tour of this garden, pointing out the different types of bamboo.

"Few people," the old man said in his ragged voice, "realize that there are hundreds of types of bamboo. This is the Black Bamboo seed." He held the small seed between his thumb and forefinger gingerly, as though it were a holy relic. It looked like a small walnut to me. "When planted, Mark-san, it must have water and fertilizer nearly every day."

He led me to a patch of dirt and pointed to it saying, "In this place, there will grow the most beautiful bamboo garden with stalks twenty feet high. But it will require great loyalty and patience from its caretaker."

I remember thinking, "Right. Twenty feet high. This guy is dreaming. I always get stuck with the odd-balls."

For the next few weeks I watched the old man lovingly tend his dirt patch. Nothing grew. Week after week, he watered and fertilized, yet not the tiniest sprout rewarded his efforts. On the day I was to return to the States, I watched him from my window. There he was, on his knees, gently pouring water into the dirt and sprinkling fertilizer onto the soil. Still nothing. I remember thinking, "Admirable, my friend. But don't be a fool—give up the lost cause."

I returned to Japan a couple of years later, and again rented the same room. As I looked out the window, I saw the old man. There he was, as I had remembered him, again with his watering can and little hand-spade. But this time, there was no dirt. In its place stood the most magnificent bamboo garden I have ever seen. The beautiful black bamboo grew higher than the roof of the house itself. At least twenty feet tall.

What the old man failed to tell me the year before was that Black Bamboo is a tricky plant. Even when watered and fertilized repeatedly, nothing appears to be happening for months on end. Even after a year, with the same process of feeding and watering, there may be no visual growth.

But in the tenth month of the second year, the seed opens. A stalk bursts through the ground, and within a period lasting no more than six weeks, the bamboo grows to a majestic height of up to twenty feet.

The question: when did all this growth really take place? Twenty feet in six weeks or twenty feet in two years?

The growth was a result of precise events staged over the entire two-year period. At any time during that period, had fertilizing and watering not been maintained, the seed would have died.

The old man knew this, though I did not. Staring at the towering stalks, it was I who looked the fool.

Systemized Marketing

To convince a prospect to think of you first, or to convince an old customer to think of you in a new way, or to get an entire organization to operate more productively, or to change long-standing attitudes and behaviors—the mental changes may require pro-active relationship-building for a number of years. And once the effort of the relationship building takes hold, results often measure in double-digit percentages. The return on effective relationship development is enormous.

Business professionals must begin to take a more systemized approach to our marketing efforts. Whether it's developing effective advertising or collateral material, creating an ad placement strategy, or even launching a public relations campaign, using a consistent, systemized approach is far more effective than the quick fix. This is true in building customer relationships as well.

Many people have told me, "If I could only get in front of a prospect then I could sell them my services." But in getting the customer's attention and interest we run the risk of losing credibility and being perceived as a salesperson. But there is a way to use a systemized approach to gaining more appointments without selling. Discovering the marketing media that is most cost-effective and addresses our target audience profile isn't enough. We need to expose our message to the audience in a way that is consistent, relevant, influential, and systematic.

Creating systems in our sales and marketing processes allows our customers and prospects to understand easily how we might meet their needs. Not every prospect is ready to buy when they receive our material, so it is important for us to have a system that ensures we will continue to influence the prospect in the future. You don't have to nag or annoy to make it happen. You need only to create interest, give them something valuable, get them on your list, and stay in touch.

It also helps the selling process to flow in a smoother and more effective fashion. Marketing systems give our sales people the tools they need to capture our company's passion and expertise. These tools can include audio tapes, videos, CDs, reports, white papers, etc. With powerful sales tools, even the weakest link in your sales staff can be far more productive. In short, a systemized approach helps us to move our clients through the ***Marketing Cycle***.

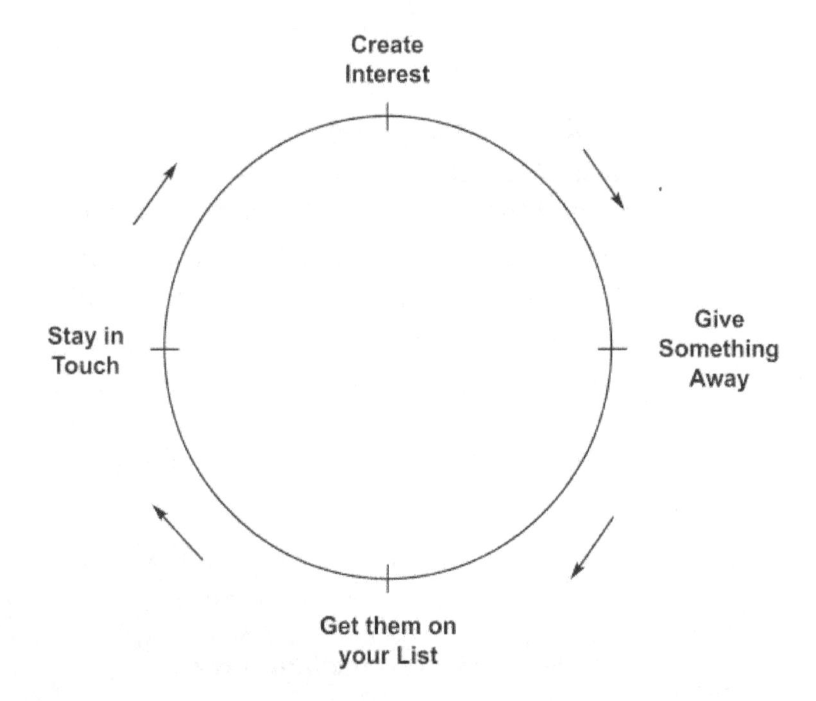

Step 1: **Create Interest**

Develop the interest of your customers by acknowledging their problems, empathizing with them, asking questions that apply to their need, and suggesting some action that reverses their risk. Forms of communication can vary from brochures, Web sites, mailers, email notices, faxes, print ads, radio, outdoor ads, and others. The message you send in your ads should also be evident when communicating in person. As marketers, it is your responsibility that everyone in our organization communicates a consistent marketing message. This includes sales staff, customer service, and all employees on the front lines with the customer.

Rules for creating interest

- Acknowledge their problem
- Empathize with them
- Questions applicable to need
- Risk reversal

Step 2: **Give Something Away**

Offer a sample or valuable information to the customer that will help them experience the product benefits or learn about how they can solve their problems on their own. This opens their minds to possible solutions that haven't yet been considered. The key is to encourage the prospect to think about their problems in terms of *your* solution without telling them about your solution, but by asking leading, logical questions. This lowers their defenses and will eventually position you as the *only* solution to their problem. Creating this kind of mind-set cannot be forced. It must be earned.

Rules for giving something away

- Remove yourself from their solution

- Educate, inform and inspire
- Deliver a consistent message in all forms
- Evangelize rather than sell

Step 3: **Get Them on Your List**

Maintain contact with the prospect on a continuing basis by getting their information. Building rapport and educating the customer happens by having them on your list. In order to effectively launch an information-based marketing program, you must craft a no cost, no risk, high benefit offer that provides prospects with an incentive to sign-up with you. You also must maintain a reliable database management system and employ a cost-effective and user-friendly list management program.

Rules for getting them on your list

- NO cost, NO risk HIGH benefit offer just to sign-up
- Reliable database and list management system
- Make it easy to cancel subscriptions

Step 4: **Stay In Touch**

In this step you must plan to stay consistently in touch with our prospect base. This involves providing information to your prospects on a regular basis. This could be monthly, weekly or even daily. The information must not be sales-oriented. It must offer very clear benefits that are customized specifically for the target audience.

Rules for staying in touch

- Make regular contact
- Information that is customized for the audience
- Provide information that is ONLY beneficial to the target audience
- Try to elimiate sales oriented information

Your Marketing Cycle

How will you use each of the steps in your marketing program?

Step 1: Create Interest

Step 2: Give Something Away

Step 3: Get Them on Your List

Step 4: Stay In Touch

Why Systems are Important in the Marketing Cycle

Think of the way a Wal-Mart store is organized. Wal-Mart is presently the largest retailer in the world with a turnover of $219 billion. Not long ago, Sears and Montgomery Ward were huge, but Sam Walton spotted their weakness and formulated his business vision for Wal-Mart. Walton's vision was to become the no-frills, low-price leader in small, rural towns.

Because of his experience as a Ben Franklin store manager in rural communities, Walton realized most small towns were, in the early 1960s, isolated from national markets. Sam realized that in rural communities he only had to beat the prices of mom-and-pop stores—local retailers—to be successful.

As Wal-Mart grew, Walton knew his firm would qualify for ever-increasing price discounts from suppliers. Plus, as sales increased, he could continuously increase Wal-Mart's operating efficiencies to drive down the firm's per-product cost of merchandising, promoting, warehousing, and distributing.

This now has become the paradigm of every Wal-Mart store. When products are ordered they flow from offshore brand name manufacturing facilities directly to every Wal-Mart sales floor with the lowest cost in the industry and with tremendous speed and efficiency. They are tracked with the most sophisticated inventory management system on the planet. Yet all this happens without a shred of fanfare or bureaucracy.

Your marketing campaign could operate at that same level of efficiency and speedy if you automate a system whereby the moment someone even *expresses* mild interest in something, they receive information that instead of being aimed at selling them product is designed to leverage their curiosity? Then, based on their area of interest they get more information and perhaps free samples? And all of this is done taking their interest at heart. Follow the 4-step Marketing Cycle and put the system in place.

Soon, the bamboo will surprise you.

Personal Action Plan

- How will you use a systemized approach to build relationships, not just create impressions?
- Complete the four-step marketing cycle on the worksheet provided.
- Make a list of critical systems that are needed in your business in order to create greater efficiency. Calendar these items for development.
- Plan some time to investigate other businesses similar to yours. What kind of systems do they employ and how can you use them in your business? What would be the potential benefits if you did?

Rule #13:

Learn the Discipline of Testing

The Edsel

September 4, 1957. A fateful day in marketing history. A brand new car debuted in showrooms across the country. Ads had spoken of the launch for months, promising an exciting new car, one that would be different from all that had come before. This successful marketing campaign had generated so much buzz that people flocked to see the car of the future; the Edsel.

What happened next came as a surprise to executives at Ford.

No one was buying it.

There are numerous reasons why: it wasn't a revolutionary new vehicle as promised; the launch date ensured that it was priced as a 1958 model, while competitors were slashing prices on their 1957 models, so it was seen as overpriced; mostly, however, it wasn't sold properly to the target audience. Ford had ignored all market research, and stubbornly stuck to their sales pitch despite the fact that it simply did not work.

Products are launched today having learned nothing from the doomed Edsel. Ignoring what the market tells us, believing we know our products better than anyone, we fail to test our products in the first place. Today we have a tremendous opportunity to test our ideas BEFORE we spend massive amounts of money turning those ideas into products. One of the most important, yet often overlooked, areas of testing is in marketing.

How can we practically test out how we are going to market a product or service before we have the product in our hands? Traditionally, the answer might be to use focus groups. Focus groups, however, carry a number of inherent problems.

- They can be prohibitively expensive
- A small number of people are not necessarily representative of the market as a whole
- That small group can give feedback that drastically changes the vision of the product, causing you end up with a watered down version of your radical idea

- Focus groups rarely do a good job at testing whether people will buy an item based on a sales pitch

So, if groups are not the solution, what is?

Use the Internet to Test

Data from Forrester Research shows that only *six percent* of U.S. Internet visitors trust search engine ads. And only two percent trust online banner ads. How do you build a brand if few people believe the ads? As I have said in previous Chapters, I do not believe that traditional marketing or advertising is effective anymore. In fact, with the advent of the Internet and breakthroughs with artificial intelligence, I believe that in less than twenty years, advertising as we know it will be obsolete.

We already have a connection to millions of potential buyers, who often times are seeking out what it is we are thinking of creating. So how do we connect with the people who are looking for our solution in order to discover the best way to market the potential product or service?

Create a smaller version of your idea, offer that for sale on the Web, and use Google AdWords to drive traffic to your site.

Let's say you have an idea for a better mousetrap. So you create a document that describes all the problems with current mousetrap technology, and how your ideas will solve those problems. You've made sure it contains enough information to let them know what it is you are proposing to create. You put this document on a Web site, and ask for feedback from people who read it.

Now to get the document in front of those people interested in new mousetraps, you can use Google AdWords. To those unfamiliar with AdWords, they are the little ads that appear on the right side of the screen when you do a search on Google. You place these ads, and every time someone clicks on your ad to visit your Web site, you pay a small fee. The mechanics of setting up a successful AdWords campaign are beyond the scope of this book but there are some great resources on the Internet.

With our mousetrap example, you may want to get AdWords for the search term "better mousetrap." This will allow you to drive a steady stream of traffic to your Web site from people who are interested in better mousetraps. Then we can measure the results of those that visit the test Web site. How many view the main page, how many download your document, how many give you feedback, and make sure you gain their permission to contact them later with new developments. Now change the presentation on this site regarding mousetrap technology. Change the text in your Google Ad. Measure how those changes affect your traffic and your conversion rate. Continue to tweak the ads and presentation for maximum conversion rates. You may even get to a point where you can sell the test document.

Once the test site has been optimized for maximum sales conversion, you may consider whether you should actually create the mousetrap. If you have been unsuccessful after six months at getting anyone excited enough to download your document, or your conversion rate is incredibly low no matter what you try, your idea may not fly with the market, and you should reconsider spending lots of time and money on research and development. If you have a successful site make your better mousetrap, however, it is obvious that there is an audience that is craving the item you want to produce. What's even better is that you have honed your sales pitch well in advance. Now when you offer your product for sale, you know what works and what doesn't work when it comes to motivating site visitors to become buyers. You also now have a large e-mail list of people who have already expressed interest in your new product–let them know when it arrives.

And thus you avoid becoming the Edsel of mousetraps.

A More Traditional Approach

Not every product or service is practical to test on the Internet. For example, let's assume that we were looking to add a new service to our consulting business. How would we go about testing the viability of this new service before we hired on staff and developed all of the marketing material to promote it?

Testing a new product service requires that we fully understand the position that our prospects *think* we occupy in the market. This will help us to understand the potential for such a service addition. As we discussed in earlier Rules of Attraction, it is not *what we do* that defines who we are as an organization but rather who our prospects *think we are.*

How do you discover what others think?

- Ask them. Just keep in mind that you may not always get the truth.
- Remain detached. You may not always get the answer you hope for.
- Start with your clients. They know you best. Remember, they are defining you in terms of their experience, not of the market as a whole.
- Be honest with them and tell them what you are planning on doing.
- Get them to focus on their vision of the future.
- Focus the questions on them not on you.
- Don't ask them if you are doing a good job or providing a valuable solution or delivering good customer service. It's not about what you're doing, it's about who they think you are.
- Ask questions about how they are affected by your business, and how they see your company.
- Ask them to paint a picture of how your companies will work together in the future.
- Ask your problem customers. If you just ask happy clients, you will not get to know what it is you are doing wrong. Seek out your disgruntled customer base. They still buy from you, and they are the ones who will be most impressed by changes you make as a result of their feedback.
- After asking a few clients. Move on to employees, neighboring businesses, associates and friends, relatives and a few prospects.

- Do not co-mingle these questions with the content of other discussion with prospects. They may feel you are trying to manipulate them or sell them. This will taint your results.
- Use different questions with different clients and prospects.
- Ask them no more that two or three questions.
- Give them a reward for answering the questions—some market information, a coupon, free shipping on the next order, etc.

Sample Questions to Help Define Your Market Perception

1. What kind of business would you say you we are in?
2. What type of problems do you think we currently solve for people?
3. What kinds of services do you think would be a natural evolution for our business?
4. If you were to need " x" series would you consider selecting us? Why? Why not? If you were going to tell someone what we do, what would you say?

Market Perception Profile

Complete the market perception profile below for each respondent to your questions. This will help you to better test the viability of new potential products or services and how your customers might perceive your market position and how it differs from your own.

Product or Service Tested:

Type of Respondent:

Name:

Company:

Their Perceptions:

How they differ from your own perceptions:

Review the "Market Perception Profiles" that you completed during your interviews, and look for the differences in how others view your test products or services. Look at the example below, then compete your discoveries.

Sample Market Perception Discoveries

I interviewed 14 prospects and clients for our weekly business coaching service. I talked to several business owners, a few of their managers and some employees who are involved in this process with our company as well as a few competitors. My goal was to discover whether it might be a good idea to hire more management coaches. I discovered the following:

1. Many felt that the experience level of the management coaches that they knew was sadly lacking. They went on to tell me that with all the middle managers out of work today, many spend months scouring the want ads unable to find the same kind of work at the same salary level and often they decide to become coaches.
2. Many owners placed great value in coaching by someone who has helped other organizations deal with much of the same kind of challenges that they were facing.
3. Others felt that having a coach gave them the perspective they needed.
4. One business owner compared it with having a mirror in which you can see yourself clearly.
5. Some talked about how coaching helps them to learn how to delegate more, how to lead their team with ease and confidence, rather than merely manage their employees, and how to feel less stressed in a demanding, fast-paced job.
6. Some of the employees told me that they felt it unfair to bring in a coach that had never done their job. They felt like some coaches were talking down to them.

All this helped me to discover that there were some very important perceptions about coaching in general which many of my prospects all probably had. The first was a potential distrust in the experience level of the coach and the second was that their employees could be resentful of a coach coming in and telling them how to do their jobs. Along with this, many placed great value in coaching and the benefits it brings.

Personal Action Plan

- Conduct the "Market Perception Profile" with one of your clients.
- Think about how you might be able to use the Internet to test your new product or marketing ideas.
- Develop at least one new product or service concept that you believe some of your clients may be interested in and propose it to them before the month is finished.

Rule #14:

Destroy Your Business

Cause and Effect

One fine summer day around 350 B.C.E. an ordinary man jumped up from his sitting position and shouted to no one in particular, "Everything happens for a reason!"

Up until this moment most people believed that the world was ruled by the temperament of various gods reigning on Mount Olympus. They believed that the events of their lives were not under their control, but rather left to the whims of hundreds of faceless gods.

The man was Aristotle and the five words that he uttered literally changed the world. In fact, so profound was his postulate that for many centuries it was commonly believed that all Western thought since that time was merely a footnote to Aristotle's "Law of Cause and Effect."

What Aristotle discovered was that we can do certain things to increase our probability of success or to decrease the chance of failure.

There are two types of people in this world: passive and proactive. Proactive people make things happen. They accept responsibility. They take their lives in their own hands. They face risk and uncertainty. They are often movers and shakers in their field of endeavor.

I often ask my students and class-members, "If you would like to double your income, raise your hand." Guess whose hands go up? Everyone's. Then I ask for some feedback on what people are doing to ensure that this is a reality. Not a peep.

Creating change is all about taking action to reduce the uncertainty of success. In other words, taking specific actions that decrease your risk of failing and at the same time increase your odds of succeeding. Heisenberg's Uncertainty Principal says that while it is scientifically possible to predict how a class of particles will behave, it is not possible to predict exactly which of those particles will behave that specific way.

For example, consider these facts:

- Five percent of Americans will achieve a net worth of $1 million.
- Twenty five percent will live to be 90 years of age in this century.

Yet can you pick the people that will?

Think about the luckiest events in your life. Trace back to the actions you took which contributed to them. Is there a connection?

Now think about the specific challenges you face in your business. Is it getting organized or establishing effective systems? Is it delegating or managing complex transactions? Is it dealing with difficult clients or employees or facilitating agreement? Or do you find yourself addressing prospects that seem to be interested only in your price?

How are you addressing these issues? By taking the path of least resistance? By going with the flow or skimming the cream off the top? Or are you fighting tooth and nail for every inch?

Are any of these effective strategies? Probably not as much as you would like. So how can we attract success rather than failure?

Attracting the Future

We are all in the process of attraction one hundred percent of our time here on earth. The question is what are we attracting?

> **Positive Attraction** - Those who talk and think continually about what they want seem to attract more and more of those very things in their lives.
>
> **Negative Attraction** - Those who talk about what they don't want and the things they fear and worry about. Or people who are angry, resentful and continually attract negative and unhappy experiences.

The secret is in managing our own expectations. We must accelerate our own expectations in order to achieve great things. In selling, marketing and managing this often means reducing a client's or employee's expectations by under-promising and over-performing. This brings about change both perceptual and actual.

In a CBS radio interview I conducted with the great Zig Ziglar, he told me, "Mark, whatever you expect with confidence—that becomes your own self-fulfilling prophecy." The most predictable and powerful motivator is an attitude of positive expectations. This is what drives change. So here's what I'm suggesting to create your own future and bring about positive change:

- Make sure that you always have room for improvement. The day you stop learning is the day that you surrender yourself to uncertainty.
- Invest some time in improving yourself daily. This may be in the form of reading, writing, listening to positive messages or even meditating.
- Recognize that improvement doesn't happen all by itself. It is NOT a matter of luck. You must decide on a specific plan for improvement.
- Put your plan in writing and post it in a place where you can see it daily. Goals unmet are merely good intentions.
- Take action every day. It may feel like a snails pace but even a little action can motivate success and create positive attraction
- Like the Ad for the Army says, "Be all that you can be." Push yourself to take that extra step.
- Believe you can and show your belief with your actions. As Thomas Edison said, "If we did all the things we were capable of doing, we would literally astonish ourselves."
- Talk and think about what you want rather than about the obstacles.

Rule 14 brings us right back to where we started in the introduction of this book: change. Today, Aristotle's "Principal of Causality" tells us that in fact we *are* in control of our destiny. We live in a world of cause and effect. We know that success is predictable and not simply a matter of luck. More than positive thinking or self-motivation, probability theory increases our chances of success. In short, we can create our own future.

I took my wife on a cruise recently. Kathy and I marveled at the magnificence of the ship. On the tour of the bridge, I noticed the officers hovering over some instruments, deep in discussion. I asked our tour guide what they were doing, and he told me: they were making a turn.

In order to turn the massive ship, they had to begin to negotiate the turn several minutes in advance.

A "business turn" requires the same sense of preemptive action. If we decide to hire someone today, in all likelihood that person will not begin to be fully productive until two or three months from now. They will need to be trained, assimilated into the company culture, and become proficient. If you want to change anything about the system, you have to think fast and move *early*. This is why knowledgeable, experienced management is so critical in small businesses today. Decision-making experience, a demonstrable skill in making proactive business management decisions is at a premium today. Companies now run lean and mean and there tends to be a shortage of management, not an overabundance. Simply put, even if there are people on the payroll that are capable of solving the problem, they are usually bogged down putting out daily fires. They are almost always willing, but due to time constraints, not able. Important long-term projects always get back-burnered to current fire-fighting. This is unquestionably detrimental to the near and long term future of the company. When we procrastinate, delaying in making changes, we cost the company much more in the long-term than a positive (albeit difficult) decision would now. The easy choice may not be the right one, but delay is in itself a choice, a kind of complacency that becomes our biggest killer.

I hope this motivates you to take action by:

- Removing complacency from your decision making process.
- Becoming the catalyst for influencing change in your business.
- Developing systems that allow the warning signs to become visible.
- Getting outside, experienced management help early on.

Creating an Attraction Plan

Is your business just a job?

Could you sell your business today?

How much do you think someone would be willing to pay?

Is that enough for you to sail off into the sunset?

What are you doing to build a property that has long-term value?

Believe it or not, most small businesses are nothing more than extensions of the owners. If the owner disappears, the business disappears. How can you make your business a property that has marketable value apart from you? It takes time and a great deal of effort, and it requires a strategic plan.

A strategic attraction plan helps the owners or principals of a business to plan to attract business growth by deliberately investing in resources that will add value and strategically dovetail with goals and objectives. It helps to define the anticipated income and expenses for each fiscal quarter as related to specific initiatives. Each of these initiatives must have an action plan including responsible parties, a timeline for completion, an ROI model, and a contingency plan in the event that the initiative needs to be abandoned prematurely. Let's take a look at the seven steps that are part of developing a comprehensive strategic plan:

> Step 1: S.W.O.T Analysis – A hard look at the company's strengths, weaknesses, opportunities, and threats. This is a critical first step because it allows us to pragmatically evaluate the company's internal and external operating variables. What factors are under our control and what factors must we accept as current conditions. This sets the stage for how to bring about change in the business.
>
> Step 2: Competitive Intelligence – We recommend using a competitive landscape grid that we teach in our "Attract More Business Program." This helps us to evaluate the competition on a number of different levels. It includes market position, product or service features/benefits, pricing,

terms, corporate personality, customer service issues, risk tolerance, financial position and growth potential.

Step 3: Values and Vision – This is where we look at the cultural absolutes against which we must weigh all of our decisions and how that plays into the ultimate vision of the company. This essentially is a "standard of care" that we want to foster in our business.

Step 4: Goals and Objectives – What is it that you want to accomplish? Where, when, how and how much? This is where the rubber meets the road in terms of growth. Few business owners spend much if any time on objectives. So is it any wonder that of the 92 percent of companies that fail in their first five years of operation, only two percent had written business objectives?

Step 5: Strategic Options - Here we simplify our options. We live in a changing world. In fact change is about the only thing we can count on. We need to plan for several options in terms of attraction initiatives. So when things change, as they certainly will, we can move to our contingency plan with fluidity.

Step 6: Action Plan – In this step we will establish initiatives and directives. This will outline a specific plan for each action item and who will be responsible for accomplishing it. What is the timeline for completion? What are some of the barriers to accomplishing it and how will we overcome them? What resources will be required and how will we acquire them?

Step 7: Metrics – How will we measure our progress? In this step we put into place the tools that will be used for measuring the effectiveness of our initiatives in the attraction plan. This includes several critical reports that every business needs to have: Sales Forecast, Cash Flow Analysis, Departmental Budgets and Product/Service Position Report. These reports must be prepared and reviewed on a regular basis.

The most important fact to keep in mind is that our strategic planning represents a *process* rather than an *event.* The outgrowth of a strategic planning process can contribute to the long term success and survival of a business enterprise. More importantly it is becoming skillful with this type of planning process which allows us to attract the kind of relationships that have value, equity and extend far into the future even outliving ourselves.

The Competitive Edge

What are you doing to differentiate your products and services from the competition? How can you set yourself apart? Marketing is not a fairness industry. Look around and you will see that the best person with the best product does not always succeed. It's because everyone is saying the same thing. Customers tend to gravitate toward not necessarily better products but those that sound different.

Fortunately, you don't need a huge advantage to succeed. Most sales are won on a very small margin. This simply means you need an edge. A competitive edge. You need a differentiable advantage that will set you apart from everyone else. The Rules of Attraction have not been designed to revolutionize every area of marketing performance. They were been designed to give you just a one percent edge.

Position yourself correctly, and that will be enough.

Personal Action Plan

Choose to live on the competitive edge:

- Earn just a little more trust
- Gain just a bit more interest
- Get just a little better at solving the customers problems
- Build just a bit more credibility
- Eliminate just a pinch more doubt
- Get a little better at gaining commitment

Impacting Others:

The Rules of Attraction at Work

The Two Poles of Attraction

The Rules of Attraction would be useless if we could not use them to impact others—clients, prospects, shareholders. The illustration below clearly demonstrates how the rules can be used collectively in order to bring about change both internally, within our organization as well as outside the organization, in the marketplace.

The figure below represents the two poles of attraction. They are symbiotic with one another in that if change does not occur within this organization, it will be very difficult to create sustained change in the marketplace. For example, if the marketing leadership within the organization is unable to create a strategy to go beyond "HeartShare" internally, they will never become a "Big Fish in a Small Pond" in the marketplace. Ultimately these two rules are dependent upon one another in order to create sustained attraction. On the other hand, if the management does create a strategy to highly target a small audience and in fact rejects the larger segment of the marketplace, they in fact will become more attractive to the smaller audience. These rules are symbiotic and complementary. In fact all 14 rules operate in the same way:

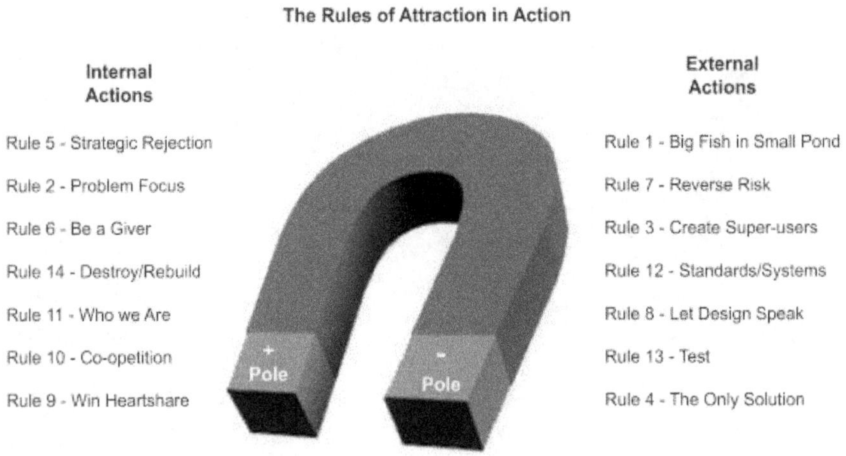

The Rules of Attraction in Action

Internal Actions
Rule 5 - Strategic Rejection
Rule 2 - Problem Focus
Rule 6 - Be a Giver
Rule 14 - Destroy/Rebuild
Rule 11 - Who we Are
Rule 10 - Co-opetition
Rule 9 - Win Heartshare

+ Pole
- Pole

External Actions
Rule 1 - Big Fish in Small Pond
Rule 7 - Reverse Risk
Rule 3 - Create Super-users
Rule 12 - Standards/Systems
Rule 8 - Let Design Speak
Rule 13 - Test
Rule 4 - The Only Solution

Companies that have used the Rules of Attraction

Numerous companies have won a greater share of "heart" in very small confined markets before becoming big players. This type of approach combines several rules of attraction. They narrowed their market, became a bigger fish in a smaller pond, used a "problem" to leverage their solution, created an exclusive community of super users and became the only solution.. When we can combine these rules we often automatically win heartshare. You can read more case studies about some of these organizations by going to www.markdeo.com/rulesofattraction.

Business Growth Assessment

Benchmarking is the key to any successful business strategy. In order to affect improvement we must understand what's working, what isn't and where we need to focus the time and attention to improve our business strategy. This assessment has been designed to focus on capitalizing on our strengths and minimizing our weaknesses. You will notice that each area of the assessment is related to one or more action-oriented items. They are the things you need to be, do, and have for a powerful, effective business growth strategy. Think carefully before you rate your organization.

Assessment Instructions

Use the criteria below to assign a score for each area on the below form:

1 = Do not have an effective strategy in this area
2 = Minimally effective strategy - needs improvement
3 = Effective strategy - but could be improved
4 = Very effective strategy - could not be improved

In order to submit your assessment, go to www.markdeo.com/rulesofattraction. After submitting the assessment you will receive some resources that correlate with your responses. These may be in the form of audio/video files, written articles, suggested books or a recommended action plan for development. In addition, feel free to contact an SBA Network consultant in order to obtain additional resources on your quest for improvement.

Business Growth Assessment

Human Quotient

Vision and Mission- There is a practical vision and mission for the company. Members of the team are fully on board with this vision. They have a clear view of where the company is headed and understand the importance of their specific role. They are excited about the growth opportunities and they make decisions daily based on achieving that vision. Team members are focused on personal improvement and several have coaches and mentors to help them achieve these goals. SCORE ________

Passion and Empowerment- Leaders and team members in the organization are passionate about performance. They feel they are making a difference. They operate in their role as if they were owners. Management communicates their expectations in an unambiguous way conducting periodic performance reviews at least twice per year, delivering honest feedback, listening to suggestions and attempting to implement them. SCORE ________

Standards and Systems- Each department has very clear standards which are achievable and understood by everyone in the organization. There are established systems and documented SOPs to ensure team members understand the most efficient and effective way to perform their work and accomplish their individual goals. Systems have been developed to accurately track and measure these performance standards. The results are consistently published and reviewed. SCORE

____

Innovation Quotient

Destroy and Rebuild- Management elects to periodically destroy and re-invent products, services or systems which have become stagnant, out of fashion or fail to meet the needs of emerging customers. This is a proactive and deliberate effort. They are consistently investigating the needs of the company, customer, market and competition to identify opportunities and to test new and unique solutions. The company does NOT compete on price alone. In fact, their products and services are typically priced higher than most competitive solutions offering benefits that competitors do not. SCORE ________

Productivity and Accountability- Departments within the company are effectively collaborating with the goal of creating innovative processes and deliverables. Clear communication usually takes place and there is little waste in terms of time or materials. Productivity expectations are consistently exceeded and technology is effectively leveraged. Most of the team members feel challenged yet still capable of accomplishing their objectives with the resources available. There is a culture of "get it right or not at all" among most departments. Individuals rather than just managers hold one another accountable. SCORE ________

Profitability and Liquidity- The company is financially healthy with good annual profits and a strong cash position. There is "profit sensitivity" among management as well as key team members. People within the organization make decisions considering the impact on the company's financial health. While there is an effort to eliminate waste, the company is not frugal about making investments in new technologies, skill development for the team and acquiring the best possible human capital available. SCORE ________

Marketing Quotient

Targeting and Exclusivity- The company's marketing efforts are narrowly targeted toward clients with the highest intent to buy. Products and services exclusively address a highly differentiated audience and few, if any competitors have significantly penetrated the markets being focused on. Sales and marketing departments work together effectively in all initiatives to communicate this exclusive claim and demonstrate how they solve the target client's most pressing challenges. SCORE ________

Marketing and Branding- The brand is distinctive and is regarded a remarkable reputation in the industry. The company has built "market advantage" and is already recognized as a leader by some of most influential industry experts. There are several creative marketing initiatives which are producing measurable results in terms of attracting new clients as well as building loyalty among current clients. The marketing initiatives include viral efforts such as buzz-building strategies, on-line marketing, creation of successful alliances and affiliates. SCORE ________

Sales and Acquisition- The sales efforts both on-line and brick and mortar are successful at attracting new clients and producing measurable results. In addition the sales team consistently exceeds their goals for referrals and cross-selling opportunities. They do NOT focus exclusively on the "loss-leader" products or services but rather expend considerable effort building value with clients for all deliverables. Sales people are skilled at developing rapport, connecting with diverse customers, probing for interest with creative questioning methods, presenting solutions in a compelling, persuasive and professional way, overcoming objections and gaining commitment.
SCORE ________

How to Evaluate Your Assessment

In order to receive your marketing attraction quotient simply go to www.markdeo.com/rulesofattraction There you can complete the assessment on-line and in a few minutes receive your score. When you click submit on the assessment your answers will be sent to the SBA Network strategic group for analysis. After being reviewed by a strategist a recommendation with be outlined and sent to you with a list of some resources as well as an action plan.

About the Author

With more than 25 years of executive management and marketing consulting experience and twelve years in the national business media, Mark Deo has had the opportunity to work side-by-side with some of the most successful marketers in the world. Because of his position as the host of CBS Radio's Small Business Hour for over 10 years he has also had the fortune of interviewing some of the world's greatest leaders in business improvement. People like Jack Welch, Morrie Shechtman, Zig Ziglar, Jack Canfeild, Seth Godin, Tony Robbins, Tom Hopkins and many more. In addition to leveraging these relationships Deo has had the unique experience of being involved with hundreds of marketing successes and failures with an extraordinary group of multi-national corporations (including: American Express, Tandy Corporation, Radio Shack, Merck, Upjohn, Rent-a-Center, Hitachi, Toshiba, Marantz Company, ASTI Pacific, Yamaha, Walker Group International, Dale Carnegie Training, First Capital Mortgage and hundreds of smaller businesses). In many of these client engagements Deo has benefited from having unprecedented and confidential access to much of the client's marketing records. This has allowed him to systematically track the results of specific attraction-based marketing initiatives and to understand the intricacies of development and implementation. Thus the advice presented in the Rules of Attraction is not only creative and effective but it is realistic, practical and tested.

Currently Mark is the Executive Director of the SBA Network, a marketing and management consulting agency based in Torrance, CA. They have implemented hundreds of non-traditional marketing campaigns for companies nationwide. He also teaches for Dale Carnegie Training Worldwide.

Find out more information about Mark Deo at www.markdeo.com

Business Attraction Resources

Learn how viral marketing can help you leverage the rules of attraction in your business by speaking directly with a marketing coach. Go to www.sbanetwork.org

Want a step-by-step method of applying the Rules of Attraction to your business? Check out Mark's new "Attract More Business Program" which includes 7 CDs and a 200page full color manual with hundreds of exercises. The program also comes with one hour of coaching from SBA Network professionals to help you implement your plan. Just go to www.attractmorebuisness.com

Listen to Mark and the SBA Network management team interview the country's leading business experts and solve client challenges LIVE, on-air. Go to www.smallbusinesshour.com

Free Bonus Material

Now that you understand the *14 Rules of Attraction*, it is up to you to put them into action. To help you get started we have assembled a powerful group of practical marketing tools. As the purchaser of this book we are making them available to you for NO additional fee. In order to receive them you only need to register at www.markdeo.com/rulesofattraction. They are as follows:

- An 18 page bonus chapter which outlines the "secret rule- Rule 15." This rule can only be used once the previous rules are employed.
- A collection of case studies which explores how other companies have revolutionized their organizations using the Rules.
- Participation in our on-line Business Growth Assessment which will help you to quickly determine where to start using the Rules to grow your business.
- Interactive PDF forms for your Competitive Landscape Profile, Exclusive Marketing Position, Innovation Continuum Chart, Market Perception Profile and more. These can be completed and submitted online. Following this, a coach will evaluate your completed forms and provide feedback.
- A step-by-step video tutorial by the author demonstrating examples of the Rules in action.
- A 20% discount coupon for the *Attract More Business Program* – a full color 200 page manual with 7 CDs in which the author takes you step-by-step through how to use the Rules to transform you business.

This material is worth **over $397** and is yours FREE with complements from the author, Mark Deo. Register your copy of this book at the Rules of Attraction Private Member Site today at www.markdeo.com/rulesofattraction. No additional purchase is required.